MAHATMA GANDHI

This book maps the genesis and development of Gandhi's idea of non-violence. It traces the evolution of the message of peace from its first expressions in South Africa to Gandhi's later campaigns against British rule in India, most prominently the Salt March campaign of 1930. It argues that Gandhi's blueprint for change must be adopted in the present, as the world craters on the precipice of catastrophic climate change, and the threat of nuclear war hangs over our heads.

A timely book for uncertain times, this work is a reminder of the value of peace in the 21st century. It will be of great interest to readers, scholars and researchers of peace and conflict studies, politics, philosophy, history and South Asian studies.

Ramin Jahanbegloo is an Iranian–Canadian philosopher. He is presently the Executive Director of the Mahatma Gandhi Centre for Nonviolence and Peace Studies and the Vice-Dean of the School of Law at Jindal Global University, Sonipat, India. He is the winner of the Peace Prize from the United Nations Association in Spain (2009) for his extensive academic work in promoting dialogue among cultures and his advocacy for nonviolence. More recently he is the winner of the Josep Palau i Fabre International Essay Prize. Some of his most recent publications are *Gadflies in the Public Space* (2016), *The Decline of Civilization* (2017), *Letters to a Young Philosopher* (2017), *On Forgiveness and Revenge* (2017) and *The Global Gandhi: Essays in Comparative Political Philosophy* (2018).

PEACEMAKERS

Series Editor: Ramin Jahanbegloo, Executive Director of the Mahatma Gandhi Centre for Nonviolence and Peace Studies and the Vice-Dean of the School of Law at Jindal Global University, India

Peace is one of the central concepts in the spiritual and political life of humanity. Peace does not imply the absence of war. It implies harmony, justice and empathy. Empathy is the key to education of peace in our world. In other words, despite the vast differences of values between cultures and traditions, it is still possible to grasp an understanding of one another, by 'empathy'. Throughout centuries, peacemakers have endorsed a 'shared human horizon' which according to them had the critical force of avoiding moral anarchy and relativism while acknowledging the plurality of modes of being human.

Today in a different manner and in a changed tone, but with the same moral courage and dissenting voice, this series on 'Peacemakers' offers the first comprehensive engagement with the problems of peace in our age, through a meticulous and thorough study of the lives and thoughts of peacemakers of all ages.

WITTGENSTEIN AND THE NATURE OF VIOLENCE
R. Krishnaswamy

MARC CHAGALL
The Artist as Peacemaker
Fred Dallmayr

MAHATMA GANDHI
A Nonviolent Perspective on Peace
Ramin Jahanbegloo

For more information, please visit: https://www.routledge.com/Peacemakers/book-series/PCMK

MAHATMA GANDHI

A Nonviolent Perspective on Peace

Ramin Jahanbegloo

LONDON AND NEW YORK

First published 2021
by Routledge
2 Park Square, Milton Park, Abingdon, Oxon OX14 4RN

and by Routledge
52 Vanderbilt Avenue, New York, NY 10017

Routledge is an imprint of the Taylor & Francis Group, an informa business

© 2021 Ramin Jahanbegloo

The right of Ramin Jahanbegloo to be identified as author of this work has been asserted by him in accordance with sections 77 and 78 of the Copyright, Designs and Patents Act 1988.

All rights reserved. No part of this book may be reprinted or reproduced or utilised in any form or by any electronic, mechanical, or other means, now known or hereafter invented, including photocopying and recording, or in any information storage or retrieval system, without permission in writing from the publishers.

Trademark notice: Product or corporate names may be trademarks or registered trademarks, and are used only for identification and explanation without intent to infringe.

British Library Cataloguing-in-Publication Data
A catalogue record for this book is available from the British Library

Library of Congress Cataloging-in-Publication Data
Names: Jahanbegloo, Ramin, author.
Title: Mahatma Gandhi: a nonviolent perspective on peace / Ramin Jahanbegloo.
Other titles: Nonviolent perspective on peace
Description: Abingdon, Oxon; New York: Routledge, [2021] | Includes bibliographical references. |
Identifiers: LCCN 2020026016 (print) | LCCN 2020026017 (ebook)
Subjects: LCSH: Gandhi, Mahatma, 1869–1948—Influence. | Gandhi, Mahatma, 1869–1948—Philosophy. | Peace-building. | Peace. | Reconciliation.
Classification: LCC DS481.G3 J256 2021 (print) | LCC DS481.G3 (ebook) | DDC 303.6/101—dc23
LC record available at https://lccn.loc.gov/2020026016
LC ebook record available at https://lccn.loc.gov/2020026017

ISBN: 978-0-367-36109-9 (hbk)
ISBN: 978-0-367-36112-9 (pbk)
ISBN: 978-0-429-34386-5 (ebk)

Typeset in Sabon
by codeMantra

TO DIPANKAR GUPTA
IN FRIENDSHIP AND GRATITUDE

CONTENTS

Series editor's preface		ix
Acknowledgements		xi
	Introduction: Gandhi as a peacemaker	1
1	Intellectual origins of Gandhi's philosophy of peace	17
2	The three pillars of Gandhian perspective on peace	33
3	Gandhian pedagogy for peace	49
4	Gandhi and the struggle for peace	65
	Conclusion: Gandhi and the future of peace	81
	Bibliography	95

SERIES EDITOR'S PREFACE

Peace is one of the central concepts of the spiritual and political life of humanity. When we study the world's religious and philosophical teachings, whether they are from the East or the West, we see that one of the basic ideals of all religions is peace. Peace does not imply simply absence of war. It implies harmony, justice and empathy. Empathy is the key to education of peace in our world. In other words, despite the vast differences of values between cultures and traditions, it is still possible to grasp an understanding of one another, by 'empathy'. Therefore, we can maintain that all cultures have a shared core of common humanity. Throughout centuries, peacemakers endorsed a 'shared human horizon' which according to them had the critical force of avoiding moral anarchy and relativism while acknowledging the plurality of modes of being human. As a matter of fact, the first step for peacemakers has always been to assume that not only there are differences among nations, cultures and traditions of thought, but also to admit that people may have different value systems which need to be understood and approached dialogically and critically. Philosophy of peace is, thus, expressed here in the idea of a 'self-respecting' community or nation which strives to remove its own imperfections instead of necessarily judging others. As a result, peacemaking is always a call not only to cultivate humility, but also to foster pluralism. Such a view is essential if we are to avoid the danger of cultural conformity and move towards the recognition of shared values of humanity and the acceptance of what Martin Luther King, Jr. called the 'cosmic companionship'. Put it differently, we can say that it would be an error to hope that we can ever achieve a truly universal vision of peace without an intercultural approach to the idea of civilization. Peacemakers have always been in favor of a farsighted peacemaking in our world which has seriously advocated the logic of solidarity and civic friendship beyond national selfishness and global exclusion. Let us not forget that all peacemakers, either man or woman, young or old, from the West or the East, were all engaged in the process of peace seeking by fighting for care, openness and empathy as constructive forms of being together. Today in a different manner and in a changed tone, but with the same moral courage and dissenting voice, this series on 'Peacemakers' offers the first comprehensive engagement with the problems of peace in our age, through a meticulous and thorough study of the lives and thoughts of peacemakers of all ages.

Ramin Jahanbegloo

ACKNOWLEDGEMENTS

I am indebted and express my thanks and profound sense of gratitude to all those friends and colleagues who made this book possible. I am thankful to my friends Dipankar Gupta, Ashok Vajpeyi, Ashis Nandy, Miloon Kothari, Neera Chandhoke and Irfan Habib for their constant cooperation and encouragement during this study. My thanks are also due to Shama Banoo Abbasi for her continuous help at the Mahatma Gandhi Centre for Peace at O.P. Jindal Global University, where the idea of this book and series saw the day. Words are insufficient to express my cordial gratitude to my editors, Brinda sen and Aakash Chakrabarty, at the Routledge Publishing House. Last but not least, as usual, I would like to record my gratitude to my wife, Azin Moalej, my daughter, Afarin Jahanbegloo, and my mother, Khojasteh Kia, for their acts of loving care and cheerful cooperation all throughout this research.

INTRODUCTION
Gandhi as a peacemaker

There is a tendency in today's world to think and to say that Gandhi's ideals of nonviolence and peace are noble ideas but unpractical and unrealistic ends. The odd thing about this affirmation is that it tends to sanctify Gandhi while rejecting his principles. However, Gandhi was not a saint, nor was he a religious leader. He was first and foremost a peacemaker, who believed profoundly in the possibility of introducing humanity to the principles of peace and nonviolence. But this could only happen if humanity could accept the law of love. Gandhi wrote in 1931: "Whether mankind will consciously follow the law of love, I do not know. But that need not perturb us. The law will work, just as the law of gravitation will work whether we accept it or not."[1] Gandhi's idea of world peace was not a dream, it was a realistic hope, armed with a dose of practical idealism, that of the global welcoming of the law of love. By saying this, Gandhi presented himself, at the same time, as an Asian who was influenced by Hinduism, Jainism and Buddhism and as a person who was deeply influenced by the teachings of Jesus Christ, Socrates, Tolstoy, Ruskin and Thoreau. Thomas Merton once wrote that Mahatma Gandhi was "an alienated Asian."[2] Maybe so, but it is not because Gandhi learnt many things from the West that he had necessarily become a stranger to his own culture and to the traditions of the East. On the contrary, Gandhi's proximity with the East and the West proved to be very fruitful and made of him, what we can call, "an intercultural Indian." Gandhi was endowed with an intellectual openness, which helped him to learn from others and as a result live up to his ideals. As such, he was not only an Indian political and spiritual leader but also the founding father of modern nonviolence.

The significance of Gandhi as a peacemaker is that he demonstrated the accomplishment of peace without war through his theory and his nonviolent action. For that matter, Gandhi believed in peace not just as a political interest but as a struggle for nonviolence. In a letter to Lord Linlithgow dated May 26, 1940, he declares:

> If there is anything in my proposition and if the British Cabinet desires it, I am prepared to go to Germany or anywhere required to plead for peace not for this interest or that but for the good of mankind.[3]

As we can see here, Gandhi proceeds against the current. For him, unlike the common opinion, peace is not the work of generals and politicians. Quite the opposite: for him, peace is the effort of the mind and the work of the soul. That is why in a letter to Edith Hunter, he observes,

> Attainment of real world peace is impossible except for greater scientific precision, greater travail of the soul, greater patience and greater resources than required for the invention and consolidation of means of mutual slaughter. It cannot be attained by a mere muster-roll signed by millions of mankind desiring peace. But it can, if there is a science of peace, as I hold there is, by a few devoting themselves to the discovery of the means.[4]

What Gandhi calls "science of peace" is simply the "law of nonviolence." As a matter of fact, nowhere in his writings Gandhi differentiates between peace and nonviolence. In a talk with a pacifist, dated March 12, 1933, he underlines the following:

> Just now a good many people are talking of world peace, promoting peace societies and passing resolutions. This is good as far as it goes. But it may not be nonviolence.

INTRODUCTION

> An army of nonviolence exposes itself to all the risks that an army of violence does. Only the latter expects to retaliate even when it is not the aggressor. An army of nonviolence runs risks without the wish to retaliate.[5]

Therefore, for Gandhi, peace is not simply a pacifist rejection of war. Consequently, from Gandhi's point of view, peace relies on the spirit of nonviolence, which is also an exercise of moral courage and disciplined self-suffering. This is, according to Gandhi, the divine aspect of human nature. More there is godliness in humankind, more it can prepare peace in the world. As Gandhi responds to an American journal:

> Not to believe in the possibility of permanent peace is to disbelieve the godliness of human nature...Peace is unattainable by part performance of conditions, even as a chemical combination is impossible without complete fulfilment of the conditions of attainment thereof. If the recognized leaders of mankind who have control over engines of destruction were wholly to renounce their use, with full knowledge of its implications, permanent peace can be obtained. This is clearly impossible without the great Powers of the earth renouncing their imperialistic design. This again seems impossible without great nations ceasing to believe in soul-destroying competition and to desire to multiply wants and thereof increase their material possessions.[6]

As we can see, Gandhi's critique of war goes hand in hand with his critique of the spirit of conquest, represented by colonialism and imperialism as the dark sides of modernity. Maybe that is why he develops his theory and practice of peace in relation with the four pillars of his philosophy of nonviolence: *Satyagraha, Swaraj, Sarvodaya* and *Swadeshi*.

Gandhi's idea of peace may seem very far removed from that of politicians, diplomats and army commanders, yet as a person who was involved with the art of strategy in an independence movement, he knew exactly which symbols to use in order to

INTRODUCTION

explain the reality of peace to his fellow Indians. For example, in his comments on a letter written on June 16, 1925, Gandhi affirms:

> The conviction is daily growing stronger that there is no peace for India, and indeed for the world, save through nonviolence. For me, therefore, the spinning-wheel is not merely a symbol of simplicity and economic freedom, but it is also a symbol of peace.[7]

Mahatma Gandhi also devoted a great deal of time explaining the moral and philosophical meanings of peace. He analysed the concept of peace through his analysis of the Hindu notion of ahimsa. He observed:

> Literally speaking ahimsa is non-killing.... Ahimsa really means that you may not offend anybody, you may not harbour an uncharitable thought even in connection with one who may consider himself to be your enemy.... For one who follows the doctrine of ahimsa, there is no room for an enemy, he denies the existence of an enemy.... If we return blow for blow, we depart from the doctrine of ahimsa.[8]

Gandhi, however, was aware of the fact that he needed a vehicle of civic struggle and mass action for his philosophy of peace. While in South Africa, he launched his movement of civil disobedience, he was not happy with the English name of "passive resistance" given to his Indian struggle. He, therefore, decided to call it "Satyagraha." As Gandhi puts it, the principle of Satyagraha existed before the word itself was coined. According to him,

> the principle Satyagraha came into being before that name was invented. Indeed, when it was born, I myself could not say what it was. In Gujarati we used the English "passive resistance" to describe it. In a meeting of Europeans, I found that the "passive resistance" was too narrowly construed, supposed to be a weapon of the

> weak, characterized by hatred, and it could finally manifest itself as violence, and I had to demur to all these statements and explain the real nature of the Indian movement. It was clear that a new word must be coined by the Indians to designate their struggle. I offered a nominal prize through Indian Opinion to the reader who made the best suggestion on the subject. As a result, the word "Sadagraha" (Sat=truth, Agraha=firmness) won the prize. But in order to make it clearer I changed the word to "Satyagraha" which has since become current in Gujarati as a designation for the struggle.[9]

As such, under the leadership of Gandhi, the philosophy of peace turned into an instrument of nonviolent public dissent and a pragmatic tool of the powerless against the powerful. However, in the eyes of Gandhi, while being an instrument of conflict resolution and universal harmony, peacemaking was also an essentially spiritual activity. What Gandhi called the "soul force" was actually "firmness in truth" and a spiritual mode of conduct. Distinguishing peacemaking and Satyagraha from pacifism and passive resistance, Gandhi suggested that the success of a nonviolent peacemaker, that is a *satyagrahi*, was because of the appeal to her own conscience. Therefore, apart from resistance to war and conflict, Gandhi explicitly assumed a fundamental moral distinction between nonviolent peacemaking crystalized in the act of Satyagraha and conscience objection to war and murder. As a matter of fact, Gandhi viewed Satyagraha essentially as an ethical commitment and a constructive political action. For Gandhi the spiritual and the political were the same. Therefore, for him, the struggle against war was at the same moral level as disobeying unjust laws: it was expressed by the soul force to uplift others. As a result, he saw peace as a universal, and not a national, ideal, in the same way that he considered the emancipation of one as the emancipation of all. He maintained that it was the duty of each individual to transform oneself by attempting to live following the principles of truth and nonviolence. In order to achieve this, one had to develop a spirit of selflessness and simplicity.

INTRODUCTION

Gandhi had a profoundly ethical view of life: he recognized neither the infallible authority of texts nor the sanctity of religious traditions, but he was also the foremost critic of modern politics and its authoritarian practices. That is to say, reading Gandhi today is unavoidably to rethink peace as a new relation between power and violence and as a way of transcending the conventional distinction between people and the State. It is a move towards a politics of the future, where solidarity of differences is not compromised by mere pacifism and democratic action is not limited by mere constitutionalism and representation. Working in this perspective, the Gandhian philosophy of peace finds the conventional meaning of power as incomplete, while problematizing democratic politics as a way of assigning a duty to citizens to be vigilant about the abuses of power by the State and to struggle against the militarization of political power in our contemporary societies. On the social side, Gandhi envisioned an ideal peace where justice is done, including for the last person. This is a common world in which institutions aim to get the best out of man.

The entire Gandhian thought in the realm of peacemaking and universal harmony revolves around the establishment of a just society. As such, Gandhi's idea of peace hinges on moral growth in man, where an undisciplined and unrestrained individualism gives its place to a nonviolent humanism. Moreover, while speaking on peace, Gandhi believed that humanity had to develop certain qualities like fearlessness, nonpossession and humility. The main aim was to restructure humans to suit to a nonviolent peacemaking society. Gandhi's repeated emphasis on service to human beings as the essence of peace is intertwined with his pluralistic understanding of humanity. In this pluralistic approach to the dialogue of cultures and faiths, he was far ahead of his time. Indeed, Gandhi's politics of peace as a philosophy of intercultural dialogue is still far ahead of our time, several generations after his death. Gandhi's idea on peace evolved through experience from a highly simplistic view to more mature, sophisticated and relevant propositions. He was not a system builder, but essentially a pathfinder towards social and individual goals. Therefore, his philosophy of peace is neither utopian nor eschatological. It is simply a critical view, which tells us what we need to do in order to go forward in the path of universal harmony from selfishness and conflict to selflessness and welfare of all. Far from being religious, Gandhi's philosophy of peace is essentially spiritual and ethical. More importantly, Gandhi's attachment to peace is more ethical than religious. Consequently, religion for him is identified with ethics rather than theology. Therefore, his concept of peace and modes and methods of achieving it, including Satyagraha and Swaraj, are not absolutist concepts. Gandhi believes that human destiny has constantly been on the move towards peace. He was a person who pursued peace in all aspects of life and who encouraged others to join him in this pursuit.

Gandhi considered peace as a dynamic element in the ethical becoming of human civilization. His effort to bridge different views of peace was matched in many ways by his approach to the many-sidedness of truth. That is why Gandhi did not reject different traditions of peacemaking; he simply affirmed what he considered to be authentic in them and thought of bringing them together in the realization of a universal harmony. This enabled him to maintain that it would not be possible to understand the concept of peace without having some understanding of the philosophical tradition of critique of violence in which it is nurtured. Gandhi, therefore, speaks of peace and nonviolence as two sides of the same coin. After all, in his eyes, they both equate with the search for truth. In other words, peacemaking is a cardinal feature of truth-seeking, simply because holding on to truth necessitates the exclusion of war and violence to ensure the supremacy of harmony and exchange over disharmony and division. That is why, according to Gandhi, peace and unity of humankind go hand in hand. As he points out, there is no way that "an individual may gain spiritually and those that surround him suffer." And he adds,

> I believe in the essential unity of man and for that matter of all that lives. Therefore, I believe that if one man gains spiritually, the whole world gains with him and, if one man falls, the whole world falls to that extent.[10]

INTRODUCTION

As we can see clearly, Gandhi saw peace in international politics as a matter of nonviolent organization of the world and interconnectedness among cultures and civilizations. As such, he was always concerned with cooperation among nations in terms of mutual understanding, empathetic friendship and nonviolent partnership. The heart of Gandhi's ethics of interconnectedness and peace was to look within one's own identity, change oneself and then change the world. That is to say, at a more fundamental level, for Gandhi, cultures and nations were not isolated entities, because they all played a special role in the making of human history. Thus, Gandhi rarely spoke in terms of a linear world history. His goal for every culture (including his own) was the same as his goal for every individual: to find the truth and establish peace. This was a way for him to open up the world to a harmonic exchange and a transformative dialogue among nations. That is to say, at a more philosophical level, Gandhi believed that peace could be achieved only if cultures and nations learn from each other.

The belief in the interdependence of nations brought Gandhi to a humanist view of patriotism. "For me," he underlined,

> patriotism is the same as humanity. I am patriotic because I am human and humane. It is not exclusive, I will not hurt England or Germany to serve India. Imperialism has no place in my scheme of life. The law of a patriot is not different from that of the patriarch. And a patriot is so much the less patriot if he is a Luke-warm humanitarian. There is no conflict between private and political law.[11]

Reading these words, we can understand well why Gandhi should be considered as a global peacemaker and not only as an Indian nationalist. As a global thinker and practitioner with a trans-historical influence, Gandhi applied his experiments with peacemaking and practice of nonviolence not only at an individual level but also in the process of the global affairs. In Gandhi's model of national and international politics, truth (*satya*) and nonviolence (*ahimsa*) were brought into a mutually interacting

INTRODUCTION

and reinforcing relation. We can therefore understand why India's *freedom struggle* was not for Gandhi a British-hating adventure. As he declared in a speech,

> I do not want England to be defeated or humiliated... It is not because I love the British nation and hate the German. I do not think that the Germans as a nation are any worse than the English, or the Italians are any worse. We are all tarred with the same brush; we are all members of the vast human family. I decline to draw any distinctions. I cannot claim any superiority for Indians. We have the same virtues and the same vices. Humanity is not divided into water-tight compartments so that we cannot go from one to another. They may occupy one thousand rooms, but they are all related to one another.[12]

The crucial point to note from this quote is that Gandhi's notion of nationalism is neither exclusive nor violent. On the contrary, he believed in a form of nationalism which includes civic friendship and intercultural dialogue. Against this background, Gandhi stresses on the significance and importance of sharing one's freedom with other nations. According to Gandhi, all national freedom is a freedom shared with other nations. As he argues,

> We want freedom for our country, but not at the expense or exploitation of others, not so as to degrade other countries. I do not want the freedom of India if it means the extinction of England or the disappearance of Englishmen. I want the freedom of my country so that other countries may learn something from my free country, so that the resources of my country might be utilized for the benefit of mankind. Just as the cult of patriotism teaches us today that the individual has to die for the family, the family has to die for the village, the village for the district, the district for the province, and the province for the country, even so, a country has to be free in order that it may die, if necessary, for the benefit of the world. My love therefore of nationalism[,] or my idea of

nationalism, is that my country may become free, that if need be, the whole country may die, so that the human race may live. There is no room for race-hatred there. Let that be our nationalism.[13]

Gandhi remains optimistic about the perspectives of world peace for the future of humanity, because he believes that nonviolence is practiced as easily among States as among individuals. As he says,

> I do suggest that the doctrine [of nonviolence] holds good also as between States and States. I know that I am treading on delicate ground if I refer to the late war. But I fear I must in order to make the position clear. It was a war of aggrandizement, as I have understood, on either part. It was a war for dividing the spoils of the exploitation of weaker races – otherwise euphemistically called the world commerce.... It would be found that before general disarmament in Europe commences, as it must some day, unless Europe is to commit suicide, some nation will have to dare to disarm herself and take large risks. The level of non-violence in that nation, if that event happily comes to pass, will naturally have risen so high as to command universal respect. Her judgments will be unerring, her decisions firm, her capacity for heroic self-sacrifice will be great, and she will want to live as much for other nations as for herself.[14]

Gandhi's argument herewith can be read as making explicit the limits of the nationalist project while insisting on the possibility of inter-State nonviolent relations as *conditio sine qua non* for the establishment of world peace. For Gandhi the idea embodying the principle of Indian unity was not the concept of *Hindutva* but that of *Hind Swaraj*. Gandhi considers nonviolent patriotism as sufficient to safeguard the national unity in India while being open to other cultures and nations. As such, Gandhi certainly rejects any form of nationalism which provides its members with the stigma of an innate racial stamp and becomes an obstacle to peace and dialogue among nations. Gandhi's humanist and dialogical patriotism is more suited to a post-nationalist situation which is fluid and can prepare the way to a perpetual world peace. According to him,

> The golden way is to be friends with the world and to regard the whole human family as one. He who distinguishes between the votaries of one's own religion and those of another miss-educates the members of his own and opens the way for discord and irreligion.[15]

Gandhi is well aware of the fact that peace is a fragile concept and it is vulnerable to nationalist justifications of violence and war. That is the reason why he refuses to define India in terms of ethnic purity or linguistic unity or some other unifying religious attribute. More than rallying Indians to combat various "Others," Gandhi's philosophy of peace and nonviolence introduces an anti-monistic and pluralistic dimension into a primarily territorial rootedness of Indianness. In this sense, it could be argued that for Gandhi, there is no sentiment of loving one's country (namely India) without loving the otherness of the Other. Gandhi, therefore, finds the foundation of his philosophy of peace in a more tolerant and diverse view of the Other. In some sense, Gandhi's appeal to a form of *civic nationalism* is in essence complementary to his impulse to support a process of *cosmopolitan peacemaking*. The first expresses the political life of citizens within a modern nation-state, while the second represents a global attitude towards peace. Ultimately, from Gandhi's point of view, both are projects with a shared vision of the common peace which is founded on the ethical primacy of nonviolence. Thus, Gandhi called into question the ideological aspects of nationalist peacemaking and its overemphasis on the racial and religious qualities of the human individual at the expense of his/her moral and spiritual virtues. It is so interesting how Gandhi defines his mission of promoting nonviolence and peace in India and in the world beyond all political and philosophical sources of hatred, exclusion, suspicion and war by calling for an empathetic attitude towards all living creatures on the planet Earth. He affirms,

> My mission is not merely brotherhood of Indian humanity. My mission is not merely freedom of India, though today it undoubtedly engrosses practically the whole of my life and the whole of my time. But through realization of freedom of India I hope to realize and carry on the mission of the brotherhood of man. My patriotism is not an exclusive thing. It is all-embracing and I should reject that patriotism which sought to mount upon the distress or the exploitation of other nationalities. The conception of my patriotism is nothing if it is not always, in every case without exception, consistent with the broadest good of humanity at large. Not only that, but my religion and my patriotism derived from my religion embrace all life. I want to realize brotherhood or identity not merely with the beings called human, but I want to realize identity with all life, even with such things as crawl upon earth. I want, if I don't give a shock, to realize identity with even the crawling things upon earth, because we claim descent from the same God, and that being so, all life in whatever form it appears must be essentially one.[16]

Gandhi's appeal to peaceful coexistence with all forms of life is a truthful and explicit expression of his philosophy of peace. This *planetary companionship* is based on an inclusive and dialogical idea of living together which disapproves all forms of human, national and religious self-centredness. As such, through his philosophy of peace, Gandhi wants to transform his Indian neighbourhood into a worldwide brotherhood. Actually, the Gandhian perspective of peace is a serious departure from the *means* of living together to the *opportunities* of living together. From this point of view, peace is nothing but a process of learning to live respectfully and empathetically in the world. For Gandhi, this comes down to accept that there are as many ways of being in truth as there are living beings on Earth. The idea

INTRODUCTION

that every living being holds a piece of truth leads us to the global consciousness about the necessity of peace on our planet. But to attain that stage, a more fundamental change is required, which is defined by our responsibility to make our world a better place. But for Gandhi, this is possible only if interdependence becomes the central philosophy of the universal human spirit. Gandhi explained this process by referring to the world as his family. "Interdependence," he wrote,

> is and ought to be as much the ideal of man as self-sufficiency. Man is a social being. Without inter-relation with society he cannot realize his oneness with the universe or suppress his egotism. His social interdependence enables him to test his faith and to prove himself on the touchstone of reality. If man were so placed or could so place himself as to be absolutely above all dependence on his fellow-beings he would become so proud and arrogant as to be a veritable burden and nuisance to the world. Dependence on society teaches him the lesson of humanity. That a man ought to be able to satisfy most of his essential needs himself is obvious; but it is no less obvious to me that when self-sufficiency is carried to the length of isolating oneself from society it almost amounts to sin. A man cannot become self-sufficient even in respect of all various operations from the growing of the cotton to the spinning of the yarn. He has at some stage or other to take the aid of members of his family. And if one may take the help from one's own family, why not from one's neighbours? Or otherwise what is the significance of the great saying, "The world is my family"?[17]

By saying this, Gandhi was quite aware of his originality and solitariness in standing firm in his nonviolent and compassionate attitude towards peace. But since Gandhi was a true believer in an interactive and dialogical world based on moral mutuality, he dismissed all forms of parochial, self-centred and xenophobic community where the universal common ground would suffer from the absence of reciprocal recognitions. Much like Tolstoy,

INTRODUCTION

Thoreau and Ruskin, Gandhi believed that a better world is possible by seeking to make space for a world without arrogance and greed. For him, peace was not an impossible task to achieve. Quite the opposite, as he put it:

> In this age of wonders no one will say that a thing or idea is worthless because it is new. To say it is impossible because it is difficult, is again not in consonance with the spirit of the age. Things undreamt of are daily being seen, the impossible is ever becoming possible. We are constantly being astonished these days at the amazing discoveries in the field of violence. But I maintain that far more undreamt of and seemingly impossible discoveries will be made in the field of non-violence.[18]

No doubt, Gandhi was furious and sad with the decivilizing process of the two world wars and the cruelty of British colonialism, but he never gave up hope for the possibility of an inter-civilizational peace, in which the East and the West would meet as equal partners in a dialogic and creative engagement. As he asserted, "If we are to make progress, we must not repeat history but make new history."[19] Gandhi, assuredly, made new history by teaching the world much more about peace than most of his 20th-century contemporaries and rivals.

Notes

1 Quoted in preface by Mark Kurlansky in Merton, Thomas, *Gandhi on Nonviolence*, Speaking Tiger, New Delhi, 2016, p. 12.
2 Ibid., p. 14.
3 Gandhi, Mahatma, *Collected Works of Mahatma Gandhi*, Volume 72, Publications Division Government of India, New Delhi, 1999, p. 101.
4 Ibid., vol. 65, p. 72.
5 Ibid., vol. 66, p. 398.
6 Ibid., vol. 62, p. 175.
7 Ibid., vol. 27, p. 244.
8 Mazmudar, B., *Gandhiji's Non-violence in Theory and Practice*, Mani Bhavan Gandhi Sangrahalaya, Mumbai, 2003, p. 9.

INTRODUCTION

9 Gandhi, Mahatma, *An Autobiography or the Story of My Experiments with Truth*, translated from the Gujarati by Mashadev Desai, Navajivan Publishing House, Ahmedabad, 1927, p. 371.
10 Gandhi, Mahatma, *All Men Are Brothers: Life and Thoughts of Mahatma Gandhi as Told in His Own Words*, edited by Kripalani, Krishna, Navajivan Publishing House, Ahmedabad, 1971, p. 188.
11 Ibid., p. 193.
12 Ibid., pp. 193–194.
13 Ibid., p. 192.
14 Ibid., pp. 195–196.
15 Ibid., p. 191.
16 Ibid., p. 189.
17 Ibid., pp. 190–191.
18 Ibid., p. 144.
19 Ibid., p. 266.

1

INTELLECTUAL ORIGINS OF GANDHI'S PHILOSOPHY OF PEACE

Gandhi certainly deserves our recognition as an exceptional peacemaker, but if anything his idea of peace was far more complex than is generally thought and quite different from that of writers such as Henry David Thoreau, John Ruskin and Leo Tolstoy, though he was inspired and influenced by all three of these thinkers. In his autobiography, Gandhi mentions, "Three modern men have left a deep impression on my life, and captivated me: Raychandbhai by his living contact; Tolstoy by his book, *The Kingdom of God is Within You*; and Ruskin by his *Unto This Last*."[1] Among the three Western thinkers, Tolstoy certainly had the greatest influence on Gandhi. Gandhi came to know Tolstoy through a pamphlet written by him called *Letter to a Hindu*. This pamphlet was written by Tolstoy in reply to Tarak Nat Das, the editor of *Free Hindustan*. Das had asked Tolstoy's opinion on the use of force and terrorism against the British, who held the Indians in subjugation. Tolstoy's response was quite the opposite. "If the English have enslaved the people of India," he wrote,

> it is just because the latter recognized, and still recognize, force as the fundamental principle of the social order. In the name of this principle they submitted to their title Tsars, the Princes, in the name of it they struggled with each other, fought with Europeans, with the English, and at present, are preparing to struggle with them again.[2]

ORIGINS OF GANDHI'S PHILOSOPHY OF PEACE

For Tolstoy, the reason the Indians had accepted British violence was that they themselves had lived with the law of violence and failed to assume the law of love. But

> if man only lives in accord with the law of love which includes non-resistance, and does not participate in any form of violence, not only will hundreds not enslave millions, but even millions will be unable to enslave one individual. Do not resist evil, but also do not participate in evil yourselves.[3]

Gandhi knew Tolstoy before corresponding with him about the *Letter to a Hindu*. He had read Tolstoy's *The Kingdom of God Is Within You* (1893) and was impressed by it. Also in a biographical sketch of Tolstoy, he wrote:

> It is believed that, in the western world at any rate, there is no man so talented, learned and as ascetic as Count Tolstoy. . . . himself a Russian nobleman, and has, in his youth, rendered very good service . . . in the Crimean War. . . . He gave up his wealth and . . . lived like a peasant. . . . He believes that . . . men should not accumulate wealth; no matter how much evil a person does to us, we should always do good to him . . .; agriculture is the true occupation of man. . . . Such is the power of his goodness and godly living that millions of peasants are ever ready to carry out his wish no sooner than it is spoken.[4]

Gandhi's first contact with Tolstoy was in the form of a letter that he wrote to him on October 1, 1909, asking permission to publish and distribute 20,000 copies of the *Letter to a Hindu*. In his reply to Gandhi, Tolstoy wrote:

> I have just received your most interesting letter, which has given me great pleasure. May God help all our dear brothers and co-workers in Transvaal. The struggle of the gentle against the harsh, of humility and love against conceit and violence, is making itself more and more among us also.[5]

ORIGINS OF GANDHI'S PHILOSOPHY OF PEACE

With his second letter to Tolstoy on November 10, 1909, Gandhi enclosed a copy of his biography written by Rev. J.J. Doke titled *M. K. Gandhi: An Indian Patriot in South Africa*.

The exchange of letters between Gandhi and Tolstoy went on until Tolstoy's death in 1910. As a result, Tolstoy's writings created a profound change in Gandhi's thoughts on peace and nonviolence. Even one can say with certitude that Gandhi's *Hind Swaraj* was written in 1909 under the spell of Tolstoy. He sent a copy to Tolstoy on April 4, 1910. Two weeks after receiving the book, Tolstoy noted in his diary:

> This morning two Japanese arrived. Wild men in ecstasy over European civilization. On the other hand, the book and the letter of the Hindu reveal an understanding of all the shortcomings of European civilization and even its total inadequacy.[6]

Few months later before his death, Tolstoy wrote his last letter to Gandhi, which was translated into English by Vladimir Chertkov. In this final letter Tolstoy expressed his despair regarding modern civilization while asking Gandhi to continue promoting his message of universal love. Tolstoy wrote:

> The longer I live, and especially now, when I vividly feel the nearness of death, I want to tell others what I feel so particularly clearly and what to my mind is of great importance, namely that which is called "passive resistance". But which is in reality nothing else than the teaching of love uncorrupted by false interpretations. That love, which is the striving for the union of human souls and the activity derived from it, is the highest and only law of human life; and in the depth of his soul every human being – as we most clearly see in children – feels and knows this; he knows this until he is entangled by the false teachings of the world. ... Therefore, your activity in the Transvaal, as it seems to us, at this end of the world, is the most important of all the work now being done in the world, wherein not only the nations of the Christian, but of all the world, will unavoidably take part.[7]

ORIGINS OF GANDHI'S PHILOSOPHY OF PEACE

From Tolstoy, Gandhi borrowed arguments in favour of his *Satyagraha* in South Africa and later in India in particular and in the direction of his philosophy of peace and nonviolence in general. As such, Gandhi equated love and nonviolence. In his model of peace, love and nonviolence had a mutually interacting and reinforcing relation. That is why in Gandhi's philosophy of peace, disobeying unjust laws came hand in hand with the love of the Other. In other words, Gandhi did not consider civil disobedience only as an assertion of one's rights but also as an act of love. As Vinit Haksar observes,

> Gandhi has an important insight, namely, that when we suffer by non-cooperation and civil disobedience (or by fasting) for our rights the oppressor is less likely to be impressed with our suffering than when we suffer (by undertaking noncooperation and civil disobedience or fasting) out of altruism or out of love for the opponent.[8]

This is the point of intersection between Tolstoy's idea of love and H.D. Thoreau's essay on *Civil Disobedience*. Gandhi read Thoreau's essay for the first time during his jail term. Interestingly, Thoreau himself was not unfamiliar with the Indian culture, since he had been a reader of the *Baghavad-Gita* and the *Uppanishads*. But the discovering of his essay by Mahatma Gandhi gave a new birth to his idea of disobedience in India and beyond. However, Gandhi did not get the idea of *Satyagraha* from Thoreau, but he was deeply influenced by him on approaching the idea of individual resistance against injustice. As a matter of fact,

> the noted American reporter, Webb Miller, a long-time admirer of Thoreau asked Gandhi in 1931 while the Mahatma was in London for the Round-Table conference, if he had ever read Henry D. Thoreau; "Why, of course, I read Thoreau" replied Gandhi. "I read Walden first in Johannsburg in South Africa in 1906, and his ideas influenced me greatly. I adopted some of them and recommended the study of Thoreau to all my friends who

were helping me in the cause of Indian independence...
There is no doubt that Thoreau's ideas greatly influenced
my movement in India."[9]

In Thoreau's essay, Gandhi found the philosophical confirmation of an idea that he already had: that the individual had to turn to his/her moral conscience as the last resort for truth-seeking. The essence of Thoreau's "disobedience," which he distinguishes from mere lawlessness,

> is contained in the word *civil* – a word of many and varied connotations. First of all, *civil* is an adjective relating to the responsibilities of the citizen, and the whole justification for Civil Disobedience lies in the idea that the man who practices it fulfills his responsibilities by demonstrating in action his disapproval of an evil law or social situation which ordinary democratic procedures will not eliminate.[10]

For Thoreau what is important in making peace with oneself and with the world is the appeal to inner sense of the moral law, which invokes the idea of responsibility towards oneself and towards the Other. In this sense, what Thoreau suggests is that to transform the world, one needs to transform oneself. Thoreau, therefore, underlines the right of conscience as a form of nonviolent resistance against injustice and untruth. According to Anthony Parel, after reading Thoreau's essay on *Civil Disobedience*, Gandhi extracted four principal ideas.

> The first concerns the moral foundation of government and the state. To be strictly just, government must have the sanction of the governed. The second idea concerns the relationship of the individual to the state. In some respects, the individual is subject to the power of the state, but in some other respects, he or she is independent of it. Gandhi agreed with Thoreau that there would never be a truly free and enlightened state until the state recognized the individual as the higher and independent power from

> which all of its own power and authority are derived and treated him or her accordingly.....The third idea concerned the need to limit government's power over the citizen. "That government is best which governs least" is the famous motto of Thoreau that Gandhi adopted as his own....The fourth idea was that the duty to disobey an unjust law requires prompt, concrete action.... Thoreau's famous dictum that under a government that imprisons any person unjustly, "the true place for a just man is also a prison", went straight to Gandhi's heart.[11]

Thus, for Gandhi, the foundation of world peace was inscribed in two major principles: love of the Other, which he got from Tolstoy, and the Thoreauvian principle of search for Truth speaking from within. As Thoreau said, "It is by obeying the suggestions of a higher light within you that you escape from yourself and ...travel totally new paths."[12]

John Ruskin was yet another source of inspiration for Gandhi's philosophy of peace. He translated Ruskin's *Unto This Last* under the title *Sarvodaya*, which is translated as "Welfare for All." Ruskin's anti-utilitarian and solidaritic critique of modern liberal self-interest made him realize that the progress of human civilization is to be measured in the scale of ethical conduct and not materialism. As the result of his reading of John Ruskin, Gandhi defined true civilization in his seminal work, *Hind Swaraj*, as follows:

> Civilization is that mode of conduct which points out to man the path of duty. Performance of duty and observance of morality are convertible terms. To observe morality is to attain mastery over our mind and our passions. So doing, we know ourselves. The Gujarati equivalent for civilization means "good conduct."[13]

At the time of writing *Hind Swaraj*, Gandhi was already deeply committed to the idea of peace, which was closely related to his ideal *Swaraj*. Gandhi, therefore, considers peace as a continuous civilizing process, which deals with self-transformation and creating an empathetic climate for conflict resolution. His strategy of replacing the great happiness of the great number by mutual accommodation of the "self" and the "other" leads to reconciliation, harmonic exchange, cooperation among individuals and nations and finally world peace. Gandhi insisted on a vital element of respect for the "otherness of the Other," which we can find in the thoughts of Ruskin, Thoreau and Tolstoy. From Ruskin, Gandhi learnt three lessons:

> That the good of the individual is contained in the good of all. That a lawyer's work has the same value as the barber's, inasmuch as all have the same right of earning their livelihood from their work. That a life of labor – i.e., the life of a tiller of the soil and the handicraftsman – is the life worth living.[14]

As for Thoreau, though he was not a mass leader, Gandhi learnt from him not to bow to the will of the majority, in case it goes the wrong way. Regarding Tolstoy, few authors in the 19th century have been as aware as him of the tempo of spiritual destiny of humankind in the midst of historical changes. But

> the world Tolstoy [saw] and [depicted was] to an increasing degree a world in which decent people can no longer find any opportunity for action...It is true that Tolstoy also preached the need for good deeds, for individual non-participation in sin and the like.[15]

Gandhi was much more optimistic than Tolstoy, and his general attitude towards the future of peace in the world was positive. He believed that it is desirable and possible to create a nonviolent society. However, he was of the opinion that peace and nonviolence will not be established without self-suffering, self-restraint and self-discipline. He truly believed that, "Civilization, in the real sense of the term, consists not in multiplication but in the deliberate and voluntary restriction of wants. This alone promotes real happiness and contentment, and increases the capacity for service."[16] For him, an indispensable means of attaining peace was self-discipline. This is what he earned from his reading of the *Baghavad-Gita*. According to Anthony Parel,

> the Gita had famously drawn the portrait of self-disciplined person, the *sthitha-prajna*, in chapter II, verses 54–72. Gandhi considered these verses to be the *maha-vakya* (the great saying) or central teaching of the entire work. From 1889, when he first studied the book seriously, till the end of his life, he used to recite these nineteen verses everyday, twice, as part of his daily prayer. They provided the daily nourishment of his active spiritual life.[17]

What also interested Gandhi in the *Gita* was the spirit of peace and the plea for harmony. As Parel notes, what we can see in Gandhi's reading of the *Gita* "is the need to harmonize action, devotion and contemplation...Gandhi wanted his spirituality to be compatible with action in the field of *artha*."[18] In other words, Gandhi was deeply spiritual, but he believed in an inclusive and pragmatic faith. On this subject, he was also inspired by Tolstoy and Thoreau, who both championed an inclusive and empathetic Christianity. Tolstoy believed that one should choose between faith and power. According to Tolstoy power-hungry beings believe that they can master history and become freer than all others. However, power-hungry beings lack the greatest freedom. The person who seeks power cannot achieve peace in himself or in his relationship with others. Inner peace, Tolstoy tells us, can only be achieved through the discovery of the living God. For him, God being life, there can be no search for life without a search for God, which is possible in human being only because he/she is naturally inclined to find God, for he/she is born innocent and without sin.

Bhagavad-Gita is the most widely read and revered book in Hindu culture. But the *Gita* has also had many readers and admirers in the West. Among the illustrious Westerners who have read it are Hegel, Schopenhauer, Emerson, Thoreau, Albert Schweitzer and many other thinkers and writers. The theoretical and practical teachings that open the book deal with the nature of action and self-knowledge. They are complemented by other interventions concerning the relationship between sacrifice and action. Afterwards, the reader is invited to meditate on the tension between renunciation and action. From there, Krishna asks Arjuna to reflect on more difficult subjects, such as Krishna's knowledge, theophany and devotion. In the course of the dialogues that make up the whole *Bhagavad Gita*, Arjuna is transformed by the spiritual teachings of Krishna, who in turn becomes Arjuna's object of devotion (*bhakti*). The core of this devotion is discipline (*yoga*), which enables the warrior to control his passions and become a disciplined person (*yogi*). The *Bhagavad-Gita* is thus presented as a search for the self, in the form of a dramatic dialogue. At every stage of the book, Krishna is aware of the spiritual conflict that is tearing at Arjuna's soul, and he guides him to the appropriate path, so that he can resolve his internal tensions. Krishna invites him not to kill but to renounce his attachment to the fruits of action. As a result of this lesson, Arjuna learns to control his action and emotions without leaving the scene of the battle. Just because the entire dialogue between Krishna and Arjuna takes place on a battle scene does not mean that the *Bhagavad-Gita* is a work of violence. On the contrary, the *Gita* advocates *ahimsa* (nonviolence). In truth, Krishna, through his teachings, explicitly rejects violence and evil towards others. Likewise, the moral doctrine of the *Bhagavad-Gita* does not apply alone to the fratricidal war described in the *Mahabharata* but to all the wars. The message of the *Gita* is, therefore, very clear and Gandhi understood it as such: that humankind should free itself from worry, for worry and anguish are the sources of sorrow and sadness. It must remain serene and tranquil. The essential thing in a human being is neither his/her body nor his/her senses, it is his/her spirit, which remains unchangeable and indestructible.

> In his interpretation of the Gita, Gandhi refers to the battlefield of Kurukshetra as the heart of man in which the two natures of selfishness and unselfishness are engaged in combat. The great need, in his view, is to cultivate selfless or detached action to the exclusion of egocentric

> activity. This is made possible for us by means of sacrifice, devotion and the service of others. Through the disciplines of such action, that is, through karma yoga, which involves ahimsa, we come to the realization of Truth or God, for to realize God is to see Him in all that lives, and to recognize our oneness with all creation.[19]

More tellingly, Gandhi emphasized that the *Bhagavad Gita* was an invitation to prayer which could offer assistance in self-transformation and self-discipline in a time of massive change in the world. As such, Gandhi maintains that prayer is

> the essence of religion and the core of a man's life. It requires no words; it is not the repletion of an empty formula. While it can be petitional, in its widest sense it is inward communion, and in both cases it cleanses the heart of passion and produces peace, orderliness, and repose in daily life.[20]

What is important here to Gandhi is the communal aspect of prayer which helps in building both the inward and the outward peace. Thus, if prayer is commitment to Truth, then peace is putting Truth and nonviolence in the service of fellow humans and other living beings.

The question that arises is whether Gandhi's emphasis on the necessity of prayer remains in the framework of only one religion, namely Hinduism, or whether it concerns all the religions of humanity? The answer to this question is simple, since all religions are in the service of humanity and in the search of Truth. There is a clear suggestion in Gandhi's writings that he rejected all forms of religious dogmatism and exclusiveness as unacceptable foundations for an approach to world peace. As we mentioned previously, peace, as Gandhi understood it, cannot be result of only one religion but the outcome of a dialogue among all faiths.

> The openness Gandhi shows to the plurality of religious traditions...indicates that he is not content to confine

himself to the small island of his own tradition and culture and consequently not recognize the significance of the spiritual insights of other religious traditions. His rejection of the right of a religion to claim superiority for itself over other religions underlines his claim that no particular religion can embody what he calls the one, true and perfect Religion.[21]

Gandhi's understanding of peace is directly related to the unity of all religions in the process of helping the helpless. This is where Ruskin's *Unto This Last* greatly influenced him. Gandhi's critique of utilitarian philosophy (which according to him minimized the dignity of human beings) pointed him towards the idea of unity of all existence. This idea is illustrated in Gandhi's ideal of *Sarvodaya* as an uplift of all fellow citizens in harmony with the ethical ideal of peace. It goes without saying that Gandhi did not consider the ideal of *Sarvodaya* as an absolute principle, but he claimed that it bound up with the search for Truth and nonviolence as universal principles. As Richards argues,

> this may point to the fundamental difference between Gandhi's ideal of *Sarvodaya*, the welfare of all, and Mill's utilitarian axiom, the greatest happiness of the greatest number, as the main principle of morality in spite of Gandhi's use of the notion of means and ends. The utilitarian axiom distinguishes the person who acts from the world in which he acts. It can be regarded as a principle apart from morality on which morality can be based since it provides a reason why it might be worthwhile for a man to act morally. Gandhi's ideal of *Sarvodaya*, is extricably bound up with ahimsa, cannot be so perceived.[22]

In other words, it can be argued that although Gandhi considered nonviolence (*ahimsa*) and *Sarvodaya* as different in theory, he did not believe that they were exclusive in practice. Actually, for Gandhi, *Sarvodaya* embodies the belief that all life is one. As a result, it is not possible to accept the belief that all universe is created as one and that all earthly creatures are equal and not accept peace as a universal end of all life. So, according to Gandhi,

> permanent peace is possible when men know themselves, and recognize their essential unity with Truth or God, and when they realize the things that belong to their peace, such as the renunciation of imperialistic designs, territorial claims and the use of weapons of destruction.[23]

Never abandoning his dedication to nonviolence and peacemaking, Gandhi stressed continuously in theory and practice the metaphysical presupposition of the unity of life.

For Gandhi, the challenge of modern civilization was to reach this unity in diversity, without any resentment or revenge. Here, once again, Gandhi established a link between the two concepts of love and justice. As he claimed, "justice that love gives is a surrender, justice that law gives is a punishment. What a lover gives transcends justice."[24] For Gandhi, nonviolence should arouse a person's sense of justice. This is how a *satyagrahi* should melt the heart of his/her opponent. The idea of obligation to disobey injustice had occurred to Gandhi prior to reading Henry David Thoreau; nevertheless, he related Tolstoy's idea of "resistance to evil" with Thoreau's civil disobedience. Gandhi observed:

> Disobedience to be civil has to be open and non-violent. Complete civil disobedience is a state of peaceful rebellion – a refusal to obey every single State-made law. It is certainly more dangerous than an armed rebellion. For it can never be down if the civil resisters are prepared to face extreme hardship. It is based upon an implicit belief in the absolute efficacy of innocent suffering. By noiselessly going to prison a civil resister ensures a calm atmosphere. The wrong-doer wearies of wrong doing in the absence of resistance. All pleasure is lost when the victim betrays no resistance. A full grasp of the conditions of successful civil resistance is necessary at least on the part of the representatives of the people before we can launch out on an enterprise of such magnitude.

> The quickest remedies are always fraught with the greatest danger and require the utmost skill in handling them. It is my firm conviction that if we bring about a successful boycott of foreign cloth we shall have produced an atmosphere that would enable us to inaugurate civil disobedience on a scale that no Government can resist. I would therefore urge patience and concentration on Swadeshi upon those who are impatient to embark on mass civil disobedience.[25]

From Gandhi's point of view, civil disobedience was not only a form of political dissent against imperialist and colonial dominations but also a figure of spiritual dissidence against the evil. As in the case of Tolstoy, Gandhi's opposition and resistance to evil is total. They both relate spiritual belief to moral duty in this fashion. As such, not to believe in the possibility of peace, in their view, is to recognize the frailty of human nature in regard to the evil. For Gandhi, belief in the act of disobedience is based on the assumption that human nature has the capacity of having moral courage and resisting the evil and the unjust. From Gandhi's point of view, the obligation to disobey was a matter of spirit and holding on to Truth. This is also how Gandhi considered *Swaraj*, or self-rule, in interrelation with the concept of Truth. *Swaraj* from this perspective, therefore, can never be achieved without being attained by the means of Truth and nonviolence. Because of this Gandhi believed in the relation between constructive work and civil disobedience. As Gandhi observed, civil disobedience without constructive work would be "a paralyzed hand attempting to lift a spoon."[26] Gandhi felt that if India is to be a just and democratic country, the constructive programme is as important as *Satyagraha* and *Swaraj*. Gandhi was well aware of the fact that peace without democracy is just another empty slogan. That is why, inspired by Thoreau and his writings, he insisted on the work of civil society next to the State in the making of democracy. He wrote:

> I admit that there are certain things which cannot be done without political power, but there are numerous other things which do not at all depend on political

power. That is why a thinker like Thoreau said that "that government is best which governs the least". This means that when people come into possession of political power, a nation that runs its affairs smoothly and effectively without much state interference is truly democratic. Where such condition is absent, the form of government is democratic in name [only].[27]

Gandhi also valued democracy as a peaceful mode of living together. Moral intervention of the citizens and decentralization of political power were, according to him, elements which could sustain peace among human beings. The point here was that ethics and politics had to work together, if the social order was to become peaceful domestically and to be able to sustain peace at a global level. Gandhi was hopeful that believers in nonviolence and peace may have a moral courage which could be a lesson of virtue to those who believed in violence, war and destruction of life. "The soldier of nonviolence," affirmed Gandhi, may give the supposed enemy a sense of right and bless him. "His prayer for himself will always be that the spring of compassion in him may ever be flowing and that he may ever grow in moral strength so that he may face death fearlessly."[28] Gandhi was convinced that peacemaking and cowardice do not go together any more than water and fire. For him, peace, like *ahimsa*, required an affirmation of courage. Gandhi, thus, considered the art of dying without killing as the true way of fighting for peace. There is something revealing in the parallel that Gandhi established between the struggle for peace and the art of dying. Gandhi's dedication to peace in the face of death was an example of his courageous attitude of mind as a Socratic gadfly. Further, one can find in Gandhi a readiness to raise the matter of dying as public policy. This is a state of mind which we can find as the background motto of Gandhi's political and intellectual life. Indeed, for Gandhi, the art of dying was very often a public act and an act of publicizing one's will to be free and to fight for the idea of peace. Like it or not, it seems that for Gandhi, to be a soldier of peace was to have the capacity, at each and every moment, to confront death as fulfilment of a Socratic life. In a Socratic manner, but in his own way, Gandhi had an examined life. His examined life was an end in itself, but it was also a way to put into question the truths and beliefs that were at the foundation of modern wars and conflicts.

Notes

1 Gandhi, Mahatma, *An Autobiography: My Experiments with Truth*, Beacon Press, Boston, 1993, p. 90.
2 Quoted in Chadha, Yogesh, *Rediscovering Gandhi*, Century Books, London, 1997, p. 156.
3 Ibid., pp. 156–157.
4 Gandhi, Mahatma, *Collected Works of Mahatma Gandhi*, Volume 5, Publications Division Government of India, New Delhi, 1999, pp. 56–65.
5 Quoted in Chadha, Yogesh, *Rediscovering Gandhi*, Century Books, London, 1997, p. 159.
6 Ibid., p. 169.
7 Ibid., pp. 170–171.
8 Haksar, Vinit, "Satyagraha and the Right to Civil Disobedience", in Allen, Douglas (ed.) *The Philosophy of Mahatma Gandhi for the Twenty-First Century*, Oxford University Press, New Delhi, 2009, p. 93.
9 Chadha, Yogesh, op. cit., p. 138.
10 Woodcock, George, *Civil Disobedience*, CBC Publications, Toronto, 1966, p. 3.
11 Parel, Anthony J., *Pax Gandhiana: The Political Philosophy of Mahatma Gandhi*, Oxford University Press, Oxford, 2016, pp. 191–193.
12 Thoreau, H.D., *Journal*, Vl. IX, p. 38 in Harding, Walter, *A Thoreau Handbook*, New York University Press, New York, 1959, p. 135.
13 Gandhi, Mahatma, *Hind Swaraj*, Navajivan Publishing, Ahmedabad, 1938, p. 82.
14 Mishra, Anil Dutta, *Fundamentals of Gandhism*, Mittal publications, New Delhi, 1995, pp. 7–8.
15 Lukacs, George, "Tolstoy and the Development of Realism", in Matlaw, Ralph E. (ed.) *Tolstoy: A Collection of Critical Essays*, Prentice-Hall Inc., New Jersey, 1967, pp. 92–93.
16 Gandhi, Mahatma, *All Men Are Brothers: Life and Thoughts of Mahatma Gandhi as Told in His Own Words*, edited by Kripalani, Krishna, Navajivan Publishing House, Ahmedabad, 1971, p. 174.
17 Parel, Anthony, "Bridging the Secular and the Spiritual", in Allen, Douglas (ed.) *The Philosophy of Mahatma Gandhi for the Twenty-First Century*, Oxford University Press, New Delhi, 2009, p. 27.

18. Ibid., p. 28.
19. Richards, Glyn, *The Philosophy of Gandhi: A Study of His Basic Ideas*, Curzon Press, Totowa, 1982, p. 33.
20. Ibid., p. 12.
21. Ibid., p. 21.
22. Ibid., p. 45.
23. Ibid., p. 152.
24. Fischer, Louis, *The Essential Gandhi: His Life, Work and Ideas*, Vintage Books, New York, 1963, p. 186.
25. Gandhi, Mahatma, *Selected Political Writings*, edited by Dennis Dalton, Hackett Publishing, Indianapolis, 1996, pp. 74–75.
26. Gandhi, Mahatma, *Collected Works of Mahatma Gandhi*, Volume 75, Publications Division Government of India, New Delhi, 1999, p. 166.
27. Ibid., vol. 62, p. 92.
28. Fischer, Louis, op. cit., p. 332.

2

THE THREE PILLARS OF GANDHIAN PERSPECTIVE ON PEACE

Mohandas Karamchand Gandhi belongs to this category of men who were both theorists and practitioners of peace. He was deeply convinced that peace was not only one of the keywords in the history of humanity but also the central idea in the centuries to come. It is in this sense that his ideas on peace and nonviolence went beyond the history of modern India alone, even though in a way it was about India, its independence and its peaceful future. Contrary to what it may seem, to say that Gandhi would never have been Gandhi if he hadn't been Indian, is not a trivial matter. Indeed, as we saw with the example of the *Baghavad-Gita*, the idea of nonviolence, in his case, has its roots in Indian culture. Gandhi became aware very early on of the specificity of Indian culture, with its strengths and weaknesses, while at the same time, he searched for points of support in other cultures to develop his thinking on peace and nonviolence. *Swaraj* and *Satyagraha* are the two mother concepts of his thinking on peace and nonviolence – concepts that are both different and complementary. *Swaraj* is the goal to be attained in the struggle for Indian independence, and *Satyagraha* is the method to achieve freedom and autonomy. However, the truth is that Gandhi considered the Vedic term *Swaraj* as an infinitely greater concept than just independence.

> "Swaraj does consist", argued Gandhi, "in the change of government and its real control by the people, but

that would be merely the form. The substance that I am hankering after is a definite acceptance of the means and therefore a real change of heart on the part of the people...After all, self-government depends entirely upon our internal strength, upon our ability to fight against the heaviest odds. Indeed, self government which does not require that continuous striving to attain it and to sustain it is not worth of name. I have therefore endeavoured to show both in word and deed, that political self-government, that is, self-government for a large number of men and women, is no better than individual self government, and, therefore, it is to be attained precisely the same means that the required for individual self-government or self-rule."[1]

Gandhi considered every nation to have the right to attain self-determination, but he also portrayed *Swaraj* as a matter of self-respect and self-regulation. Therefore, as Gandhi understood, any nation that acquired *Swaraj* would at the same be able to guarantee the basic rights of the citizens. This was possible because Gandhi defined *Swaraj* not only as a political concept but also as a moral foundation to the public action of the citizens. In addition, what Gandhi did was to make *Swaraj* a bridge between the private and the public. As such, from his point of view an autonomous individual had to correspond to an autonomous community. Therefore, with Gandhi *Swaraj* became an interface between the political and the ethical, a culture of the self which was also a communitarian project.

From Gandhi's point of view, *Swaraj* incorporated many aspects of his philosophy, including *Satyagraha*, *Swadeshi*, *Sarvodaya* and more specifically the problems of education, women, spinning and Hindu-Muslim unity. As for the different meanings of *Swaraj* put into practice by Gandhi, we can refer to his response to a correspondent on October 20, 1929, in Navajivan. Gandhi wrote:

> The writer has narrowed down the very meaning of swaraj itself. The gentleman seems to believe that swaraj means the transfer of power from British hands to Indian

hands. To my mind swaraj means regulated power in the hands of thirty crores of people. Where there is such rule, even a young girl will feel safe and, if the imagination of a poet is correct, animals like dogs, etc. who live among human beings will have a similar feeling of safety. We shall have to arrive at various basic decisions in regard to swaraj, because under swaraj such decisions are not subject to officials in power but are based on truth and justice. I have succinctly called this kin of swaraj Ramarajya.[2]

For Gandhi, Ramarajya was considered as the ideal state. Far from being a theocratic state or a moralistic city, Gandhi imagined and portrayed it as an integral democracy. Therefore, Gandhi made an acute distinction between the religious government of the Hindus and a sovereignty of the people based on ethical citizenry. As he explained in *Young India* on May 28, 1931, "By Ramaraj I do not mean Hindu *raj*. I mean by Ramaraj Divine *raj*, the Kingdom of God...The ancient ideal of Ramaraj is undoubtedly one true democracy."[3] The essential in Gandhi's theory of *Swaraj* is the process of self-rule. His belief was that Indians should learn to rule themselves. Thus, parliamentary democracy would be the end result of this self-rule. In 1920, Gandhi suggested that his "Swaraj is the Parliamentary Government of India in the modern sense of the term."[4] Over the next two decades Gandhi developed a theory and practice of *Swaraj* which one can find in germ in *Hind Swaraj*. As in his seminal book, Gandhi came to distinguish between *Swaraj* and "independence." As Bhikhu Parekh observes in his book *Colonialism, Tradition and Reform*, for Gandhi,

> unlike independence, a negative and legal concept, swaraj wasa positive and cultural concept signifying full autonomy or self-determination...Swaraj was a form of collective integrity, a community's mode of being true to itself and running its affairs in harmony with its deepest truth. For Gandhi, swaraj was the ultimate ideal of every territorially organised society. Independence was it

necessary but by no means sufficient condition and was desirable only because a country forced to live by its ruler's truth remained untrue to itself.[5]

Gandhi believed that the term "independence" did not have the spiritual and the moral weight of *Swaraj*. After all, he regarded *Swaraj* as being selfless and incorruptible. But more important than all, *Swaraj* meant to him freedom for the poorest of all Indians. It also represented "the vesting of the ultimate authority in the peasant and the labourer and not the mere transference of power from the white bureaucrat to the brown bureaucrat."[6]

As a matter of fact, Gandhi was convinced that independence gained through violence was incapable of producing citizens with necessary moral qualities. That is why he considered *Swaraj* as a work of moral courage and terrorism as a method practised by cowards. He, therefore, decided to offer a new reading of the Hindu texts (as we saw in the case of the *Baghavad Gita*) and "to take over terms familiar to his audience and to define them in the way he thought proper without much worrying about their conventional meanings."[7] For Gandhi, then, *Swaraj* meant creating or restoring self-dignity and self-respect for a nation which had suffered domination and violence. In response to his critics, he affirmed the following in 1931:

> Of course, you will say that India free can become a menace herself. But let us assume she will behave herself with her doctrine of nonviolence if she achieves her freedom through it, and for all her bitter experience of being a victim of exploitation.[8]

Since his first writings in South Africa, and especially in *Hind Swaraj*, Gandhi positioned himself against those who believed that peace will follow logically the independence of India even if terrorism and violence are practised against the British. In addition to this, Gandhi was well aware of the tense dialectic between his project of *Swaraj* and political and religious violence in India. Gandhi's opposition to the creation of a religious State, either Hindu or Muslim, was grounded in his conception of perpetual peace as the ultimate end of *Swaraj*. Though Gandhi defined peace, beyond the political and polemological frontiers, as a spiritual liberation, he could not possibly restrict *Swaraj* to a homogeneous religious nation. For Gandhi, *Swaraj* meant building a nation without ill will and selfishness: the same moral qualities he prescribed for world peace. Given his approach of *Swaraj* as a form of active love, it implied necessarily the self of a nation and the otherness of the Others. Therefore, it implied an Indian nation which did not engage in any form of violence against its opponents and critics. As a result, Gandhi saw the true *Swaraj* being established in relation with a peaceful and moral equivalence between the Indians of all religions, languages and opinions, but also between the Indian nation and other nations. That is why the moral worth of *Swaraj* was characterized by its appeal to *Satyagraha* as a form of nonviolent warfare. Gandhi knew well that the end of violence did not come with the end of British rule. The Partition and what followed in India in the past seven decades showed us that he was right. He wrote: "Of what value is swaraj without nonviolence? The way to destroy *adharma* is to establish dharma...Adharma can be destroyed only through dharma. If there is no one to submit to oppression, there can be no oppression."[9] Gandhi invited Indians to live in peace with all the other religions, cultures and nations, according to its own dharma. This was not possible without self-purification. As stated by Gandhi,

> One's respective dharma towards one's self, family, nation and the world cannot be divided into watertight compartments. The harm done to oneself of one's family cannot bring about the good of the nation. Similarly, one cannot benefit the nation by acting against the world at large... Therefore, it all starts from self-purification. When the heart is pure, from moment to moment one's duty becomes apparent effortlessly.[10]

Gandhi developed his *Satyagraha* not only as a nonviolent weapon against South African racism and later in opposition to British colonialism but also as a nonviolent mode of life. Nobody had heard of nonviolence in political struggle before Gandhi's campaigns in South Africa.

> The overwhelming impact of ahimsa on Gandhi's nationalism was triggered by his reading of the New Testament; thus he Christianised the meaning of the word and gained a sympathetic audience of Christians throughout the world. But Gandhi solidly anchored the Christian injunction in the Hindu tradition. Ahimsa and nationalism in the garb of civil resistance gave birth to a new concept and word coined by Gandhi. "Satyagraha" is the name he gave to his weapon of political nonviolence and, incidentally, to 'way of life' he thus promoted.[11]

As such, Gandhi's perception of politics and peace was transformed through his discovery of *Satyagraha* as a mode of resistance against the British imperial power. However, strangely as it may appear, "Satyagraha was not only an appeal to the British constitution, it was also an appeal to the British conscience...It was based upon a deep understanding of British history and character."[12] For Gandhi, the understanding of the British colonial rule went hand in hand with a new approach to modern civilization. In that sense, what counted for Gandhi was to apply Satyagraha as a means to get to the appropriate end, *Swaraj*, in order to get to a new definition of civilization. But,

> Satyagraha was not added to the repertoire of Gandhi's methods of agitation in South Africa until 1906. Its adoption represented a particular phase in Gandhi's mental evolution which was induced by his increasing interest in religion and his study of writers like Tolstoy, John Ruskin and Henry David Thoreau. It was dictated by the needs of the situation in South Africa... But it was not entirely uninfluenced by developments outside South Africa, notably those in Ireland, England and India.[13]

PILLARS OF GANDHIAN PERSPECTIVE ON PEACE

Gandhi practiced *Satyagraha* not merely as a means of taming violence but also as an effective way of suffering for the violence of others without inflicting any harm on them. That is why, by practicing *Satyagraha*, Gandhi was working for the uplift of the moral spirit of his fellow humans while promoting the welfare of his country. Next to *Swaraj*, *Swadeshi* and *Sarvodaya*, Gandhi presented *Satyagraha* as a philosophy of life. Much like Socrates, Gandhi saw nonviolent approach to life as a mode of questioning reality of his time. He believed that this task of questioning and objecting would enlighten the conscience of human beings and appeal to their hearts. And this, Gandhi felt, was the ethical foundation of living together. This was the process of self-transformation that individuals had to go through in order to attain *Swaraj* as an essential art of self-governing. Thus, in the eyes of Gandhi, *Swaraj* as self-determination was also necessarily a quest for Truth. "The moment one deviated from truth, the ethical conduct of life, one could not be called a satyagrahi, the truth seeker."[14] Surely, from Gandhi's point of view, the dynamics of peace ran along these lines. The practice of *Satyagraha*, therefore, represented an exercise of speaking truth to power and also an ability to participate in a social and political struggle without having a desire for revenge or hatred. That is the reason why Gandhi believed that "there is no such thing as defeat in satyagraha." As he wrote in 1929, "once a satyagrahi has chalked out his path, he never retreats from it."[15] A year later he described new features of his theory and practice of *Satyagraha*. He observed,

> Satyagraha literally means insistence on truth. This insistence arms the votary with matchless power. This power or force is connoted by the word satyagraha. Satyagraha, to be genuine, may be offered against parents, against one's wife or one's children, against rulers, against fellow-citizens, even against the whole world. Such a universal force necessarily makes no distinction between kinsmen and strangers, young and old, man and woman, friend and foe. The force to be so applied

can never be physical. There is in it no room for violence. The only force of universal application can, therefore, be that of ahimsa or love. In other words, it is soul force.[16]

Gandhi viewed *Satyagraha* as a substantial ethical commitment which called on the moral courage of the individual in order to resist untruth and injustice in a transparent manner. Consequently, Gandhi considered the work of politics as an act of transparency. He mentioned it clearly in his response to questions asked from him on civil disobedience. "A satyagrahi," he replied, "has no secrets to keep from his opponent or so-called enemy."[17] As a result, for Gandhi the ultimate achievement of transparent citizenry for a *satyagrahi* was to be able to convince the opponent of its wrongdoing. "Satyagraha not being a war of violence," wrote Gandhi,

> but being a war of conversion and conviction...I know for certain that if we can ensure reform from within, the other will follow as day follows night. I am equally certain that no reform from without can avail without reform from within.[18]

According to Gandhi, it is only by pursuing an ethical life that *satyagrahis* could achieve a genuine *Swaraj* as a basic harmony between the act of truth-seeking (*Satyagraha*), nonviolence (*ahimsa*) and economic self-sufficiency (*Swadeshi*). In March 1925, Gandhi wrote the following about his politics of *Swadeshi*:

> My definition of swadeshi is well known. I must not serve distant neighbour at the expense of the nearest. It is never vindictive or punitive. It is in no sense narrow, for I buy from every part of the world what is needed for my growth. I refuse to buy from anybody anything, however nice or beautiful if it interferes with my growth or injures those whom Nature has made my first care. I buy healthy literature from every part of the world. I buy surgical instruments from England, pins and pencils from Austria and watches from Switzerland. But I will

> not buy an inch of the finest cotton fabric from England
> or Japan or any other part of the world because it has injured and increasingly injures the millions of the inhabitants of India. I hold it to be sinful for me [not] to buy the
> cloth spun and woven by the needy millions of India's
> paupers and to buy foreign cloth, although it may be superior in quality to the Indian hand-spun. My swadeshi,
> therefore, chiefly centres round the hand-spun khaddar
> and extends to everything that can be and is produced
> in India. My nationalism is as broad as my swadeshi.
> I want India's rise so that the whole world may benefit. I
> do not want India to rise on the ruin of other nations.[19]

It is well known that Gandhi's choice of *Khadi* was a symbolic gesture in order to unify Indians behind the home manufacture. As a matter of fact, one of Gandhi's fundamental actions in empowering *Swaraj* and fighting the British Raj was to speak the language of nonviolent resistance instead of practicing the language of domination of the colonizers. As Peter Gonsalves points out,

> *Swadeshi* in the pursuit of *swaraj* for all, beginning with
> the most underprivileged of India's outcastes was not
> merely a shrewd political ploy to drive out the British; it
> was Gandhi's whole being – his thinking, living, acting
> and his manner of presenting himself in public places. He
> epitomized this unity of purpose and action in his frail
> body, draped at the waist in simple hand-spun *khadi*.[20]

For Gandhi, the *Khadi* spoke louder than hundreds of political slogans. It became a symbol of protest, defiance and unity. In the making and wearing of the *Khadi*, Gandhi found a symbiosis between *Swaraj*, *Satyagraha* and *Swadeshi*. Not only *Khadi* eliminated distinctions and inequalities but it also appeared as a defiance of the laws of the British colonizers. According to Gandhi, the key to *Swaraj* was not in London but in the *Khadi*. That is why Gandhi invited all the Indians to spin. Spinning was not only a political manifest; it was also an educational task. As such,

PILLARS OF GANDHIAN PERSPECTIVE ON PEACE

Gandhi attributed a *paideic* nature to *Swaraj* and *Swadeshi*. We can see this formulated in the Declaration of Trust of Navajivan. The aim and object of Navajivan Trust was

> to propagate peaceful means for the attainment of Hind Swaraj, i.e. swaraj for India, by educating the people through cultivated and enlightened workers devoted to the Gujarati language who desire to identify themselves with the life of Gujarat through the means of Gujarati and to serve India in this pure manner.[21]

However, Gandhi was well aware of the fact that *Swaraj* and literacy were two different things. "If we have to wait," he said, "until crores of people have gained a knowledge of the alphabet in order to win swaraj, attainment of the letter will become almost an impossibility."[22] Gandhi's point was that India had been enslaved because Indians had accepted voluntarily to become slaves. The aim of *Swadeshi* was, therefore, to teach Indians to self-govern themselves. Gandhi's hope for a free India with self-governing Indians found its expression in his idea of self-sacrifice and love. "If India adopted the doctrine of love as an active part of her religion and introduced it in her politics, Swaraj would descend upon India from heaven."[23] Gandhi's idea of socio-economic decentralization, exemplified by his Constructive Program, was actually a whole project of humanization of everyday life for all those ordinary Indians, who had no possibility of uplifting the quality of their lives. There was no question for Gandhi that democracy would be constructed by some on behalf of others. Gandhi believed that his ideas of Constructive Program could be implemented only in a country where democracy and individual rights were respected. However, this called for a modification of attitudes and transformation of values. Moving against the tide, Gandhi carved a theory of democracy that laid the foundation of a meaningful citizen participation and peacemaking. Gandhi's idea of democracy rests upon the premise that every citizen is responsible for every act of the State, but the ultimate allegiance of a citizen is towards self-government and the State. Yet, Gandhi was aware that democracy was achieved through respect of the just and disobedience of the unjust. Gandhi considered moral resistance as the indicator of a healthy democracy. A reminder that authoritarianism is often caused by a docile and obedient mind, and it takes very little for a democracy to slip into the tyrannical mode. This act of disobedience is not a random or an unpremeditated decision. Gandhi saw it as a careful reflection of citizens on the limits of power and the possibility of peacemaking. Gandhi was thinking in terms of reflective and critical citizens who dare to speak back to power. This is what *Swaraj* is all about for Gandhi: a shared search for Truth, which defines freedom as an act of becoming. As Gandhi noted,

> I hope to demonstrate that real *swaraj* will come not by the acquisition of authority by a few but by the acquisition of the capacity by all to resist authority when abused. In other words, *swaraj* is to be attained by educating the masses to a sense of their capacity to regulate and control authority.[24]

Thus, Gandhi extended his ideal of *Swaraj* to the capacity for self-rule of the free and autonomous citizens of democracy. Democracy, to be worthy of obedience, he observed, must be structured so that every citizen can question and disobey unjust laws and institutions. Gandhi saw peacemaking as part of the process of democracy building. Thus, the Gandhian moment of peace is a distinctive experience of political action and an experimental moment of nonviolence as an emancipatory praxis. This is where peacemaking joins *Swaraj*, *Satyagraha*, *Sarvodaya* and *Swadeshi*. For Gandhi, the process of peacemaking generates new practices of empathetic pluralism, as well as new modes of individual and collective self-rule to reconstitute the political realm of interconnectedness.

Consequently, Gandhi saw peace as a form of shared sovereignty and as a creative and enlightened democracy. As such, his nonviolent approach to peace was formulated as the respect for the principle of self-rule and the acceptance of sharing power with the poorest and the most ordinary citizen. This is where we can see the interconnection between the Gandhian goal of spiritualizing politics, promoting an intercultural dialogue and promoting values such as responsibility and civility, and peacemaking. Seeking to provide humanity with an alternative vision of peace, Gandhi's critique of war and violence combined a rejection of the modern theory of power represented by thinkers like Machiavelli and Hobbes, with a re-reading and re-writing of the Indian tradition of social and political institutions. Furthermore, Gandhi articulated his alternative vision of peace far from the dark side of modernity and close to the process of political mobilization of the subalterns. As a result, Gandhi's answer to modern conflicts and wars was nonviolence as a moral conviction and as an anthropology.

As evident, *Hind Swaraj* was the most Gandhian creative response to the moral perversion of the modern warfare. In a comment in 1921, Gandhi explained why he wrote this book. "It was written," he said,

> in answer to the Indian school of violence, and its prototype in South Africa. I came in contrast with every known Indian anarchist in London. Their bravery impressed me, but I feel that their zeal was misguided. I felt that violence was no remedy for India's ills, and that her civilization required the use of different and higher weapon for self-protection. The Satyagraha of South Africa was still an infant hardly two years old. But it had developed sufficiently to permit me to write of it with some degree of confidence... [*Hind Swaraj*] teaches the gospel of love in the place of that of hate. It replaces violence with self-sacrifice. It pits soul-force against brute force.[25]

In other words, from Gandhi's point of view, *Hind Swaraj* served three purposes: a critique of modern civilization, which Gandhi considered immoral, utilitarian and materialistic; engaging a dialogue with violence-oriented Indian nationalists; and last but not least laying the principal theoretical pillars of peacemaking. *Hind Swaraj* tried to provide us with an ethical response to the violent and unethical basis of Western civilization. Critical of instrumental rationality, as an expression of modern civilization, Gandhi defended his view of what could be a true civilization based on *dharma*. He maintained that a civilization in search of Truth and aware of the need to live and act in accordance with moral law is a civilization on the "path of duty." As Tridip Suhrud observes,

> For Gandhi, the essential character of modern civilization is not represented by either the Empire, or the speed of railways, the contractual nature of society brought by Western law, nor by the vivisection practiced in modern medicine. It is also not represented by use of violence as a legitimate means of expressing political dissent and obtaining political goals, even though these are significant makers of modern civilization. The essential character of modern civilization is represented by denial of a fundamental possibility, that of knowing oneself.[26]

This search for oneself in relation with the Other is another basic pillar in Gandhian thought that makes the quest for peace viable. Clearly, Gandhi's *Hind Swaraj* was a critical response against the socio-political and psycho-cultural circumstances of colonial and imperial dominations, which had made many non-Western nations, including India, alien to their own civilizational selves and servile to the Others. As a result, Gandhi came up with a new definition of the autonomous individual as opposed to servile individual in *Hind Swaraj*. According to Bidyut Chakrabarty,

> Unlike the Enlightenment conceptions of individualism, which separate individuals from their tradition and vice versa, Gandhi provided a theory of the autonomy of individuals, designed to empower individuals within their traditions and community. By homogenizing individuals, Western rationalism, defined as part of modernity, tended to gloss over the diverse nature of human beings due to their socio-economic and cultural roots…. What was creative in Gandhi's response was the idea that, although Western modernity was unavoidable in

a colonial context, it needed to be reinvented by taking into account the specificities of the immediate context of the Indian reality.[27]

Seeking to provide an alternative to Western modernity, Gandhi preferred to strike an emotional chord with the Indian masses by showing them the "Indianness" of his model of anti-domination and peace. However, what helps us to understand Gandhi as a peacemaker is the political representation of this "Indianness" in its plurality and diversity. For Gandhi, Indian self-rule was Indian people's self-fulfilment regardless of their religious, linguistic or ethnic differences. Therefore, Gandhi's plural and civic nationalism against foreign rule was not accompanied by an exclusive and one-dimensional view of "Indianness." As such, the basic model that Gandhi provided in *Hind Swaraj* continued to remain as a constant referent in his later approaches to the idea of world peace. In it is the context of such a theoretical approach that Gandhi continued to believe in the possibility of a Hindu-Muslim unity in India. He believed that the British had established their colonial rule by taking advantage of the quarrels between the Muslims and the Hindus. He declared:

> I have no doubt that if the British rule which divides us by favouring one or the other as it suits the Britishers were withdrawn today, Hindus and Muslims would forget their quarrels and live like brothers which they are. But supposing the worst happened and we had a civil war, it would last for a few days or months and we would settle down to business. In status, we are equal. Immediately, the British rule is really ended, we shall grow as never before. You don't know how the [British] rule has stunted the nation.[28]

Though Gandhi's response to the communal violence in India and later to the Partition may appear naïve and unrealistic, it should be pointed out that it remained a transformative vision with a utopian character, which were couched in ethical and spiritual terms whereby peace and nonviolence were always privileged over war and conflict. Gandhi was insistent on communal peace as much as on world peace. Ultimately, he did not see Hinduism and Islam as two opposing religions but as parts of the same Truth that we all try to seek in our experiments in life. As he remarked:

> There is nothing on earth that I would not give up for the sake of the country excepting of course two things and two only, namely, truth and non-violence. I would not sacrifice the two for all the world. For to me Truth is God and there is no way to find Truth except the way of non-violence. I do not seek to serve India at the sacrifice of Truth or God. For I know that a man who forsakes Truth can forsake his country, and his nearest and dearest ones.[29]

Notes

1. Gandhi, Mahatma, *Selected Political Writings*, op. cit., p. 100.
2. Gandhi, Mahatma, *Collected Works of Mahatma Gandhi*, Volume 42, Publications Division Government of India, New Delhi, 1999, p. 22.
3. Dhawan, Gopinath, *The Philosophy of Mahatma Gandhi*, Navajivan Publishing, Ahmedabad, 1957, p. 294.
4. Quoted in Dhawan, Gopinath, op. cit., p. 294.
5. Parekh, Bhikhu, *Colonialism, Tradition and Reform: An Analysis of Gandhi's Political Discourse*, Sage Publications, New Delhi, 1989, p. 158.
6. Dhawan, Gopinath, op. cit., p. 293.
7. Parekh, Bhikhu, op. cit., p. 116.
8. Fischer, Louis, *The Essential Gandhi*, op. cit., p. 197.
9. Gandhi, Mahatma, *Collected Works of Mahatma Gandhi*, Volume 19, Publications Division Government of India, New Delhi, 1999, p. 11.
10. Gandhi, Mahatma, *The Essential Writings of Mahatma Gandhi*, edited by Iyer, Raghavan, Oxford University Press, New Delhi, 1993, p. 183.
11. Panter-Brick, Simone, *Gandhi and Nationalism: The Path to Indian Independence*, Viva Books, New Delhi, 2012, p. 57.
12. Gandhi, Mahatma, *Indian Home Rule* [Hind Swaraj], Introduction by Mehrotra, S.R., Promilla&Co. Publishers, New Delhi, 2009, p. 55.

13 Ibid., p. 54.
14 Samaddar, Ranabir, "Gandhi and Tagore", in Pfostel, Eva (ed.) *Between Ethics and Politics: Gandhi Today*, Routledge, New Delhi, 2014, p. 101.
15 Gandhi, Mahatma, *The Collected Works of Mahatma Gandhi*, op. cit., vol. 42, p. 129.
16 Ibid., vol. 42, p. 491.
17 Ibid., vol. 42, p. 482.
18 Gandhi, Mahatma, *The Collected Works of Mahatma Gandhi*, op. cit., vol. 26, p. 243.
19 Ibid., pp. 278–279.
20 Gonsalves, Peter, *Clothing for Liberation: A Communication Analysis of Gandhi's Swadeshi Revolution*, Sage Publications, New Delhi, 2010, p. 126.
21 Gandhi, Mahatma, *The Collected Works of Mahatma Gandhi*, op. cit., vol. 42, p. 211.
22 Ibid., p. 281.
23 Gandhi, Mahatma, *The Selected Works of Mahatma Gandhi*, Volume IV, edited by Narayan, Shriman, Ahmedabad, Navajivan Publishing House, 1968, p. 97.
24 Gandhi, Mahatma, *All Men Are Brothers*, op. cit., p. 221.
25 Gandhi, Mahatma, *The Collected Works of Mahatma Gandhi*, op. cit., vol. 19, p. 277.
26 Suhrud, Tridip, "Gandhi's Key Writings: In Search of Unity", in Parel, Anthony & Brown, Judith M. (ed.) *The Cambridge Companion to Gandhi*, Cambridge University Press, New Delhi, 2011, p. 73.
27 Chakrabarty, Bidyut, *Social and Political Thought of Mahatma Gandhi*, Routledge, Oxon, 2006, p. 175.
28 Gandhi, Mahatma, *Harijan*, May 4, 1940, quoted in Chakrabarty, Bidyut, op. cit., p. 121.
29 Gandhi, Mahatma, *All Men Are Brothers*, op. cit., p. 133.

3

GANDHIAN PEDAGOGY FOR PEACE

Gandhi had an immense interest in international politics. As a result, he was always following global developments closely and acutely. During his life he chose to enter wars, not in order to fight but as a matter of duty. According to Simone Panter-Brick,

> Gandhi chose to enter wars even when he did not have to. Nobody asked him to put on an army uniform. In fact, it was not that easy to have his services accepted by the Army. But the point was not whether he liked it or not, but whether this was or was not his duty.[1]

Gandhi didn't think that violence was beneficial for the individual. Unlike Frantz Fanon, who analysed violence as a liberating force for the colonized against the colonizer, Gandhi's arguments were directed against the nature of power itself. For Gandhi, brute force did not liberate slaves from servility, since no real transformation to freedom would follow. It follows that for Gandhi no independence could be won through violence. He had three interdependent arguments for this.

> One: howsoever urgent the need for violence, it is neither pragmatic nor productive.... Two: Gandhi's rejection of violence originates in an epistemological argument on the nature of truth. The production and reproduction of violence follow the absolute conviction that we, and only we, are in possession of the truth, and that the other's

> truth is necessarily false... But truth to Gandhi is as elusive as the proverbial will o' the wisp. It escapes the moment we think we have accessed it... Three: Gandhi's rejection of violence is ontological, grounded in his belief in the philosophy of *advaita* or non-dualism...Since the other is part of you, any act that causes harm to others injures you as well. The normative argument, the epistemological argument, and the ontological argument build up a formidable case against violence.[2]

Gandhi's approach to peace was an integral part of his philosophy of nonviolence. However, as it was mentioned previously, for Gandhi, peace did not mean deferment of war. According to Gandhi, peace can only exist when there is no more violence among nations. Moreover, Gandhi was far from being a simple pacifist, because he applied his philosophy of nonviolence to all spheres of life and not only war. Now, the million-dollar question is the following: Could Gandhi's nonviolence have been effective with dictators like Hitler or Stalin? This is a question which was asked from Gandhi during his lifetime. His answer was always strong and clear. For Gandhi, such an argument presupposed "that the dictators like Mussolini and Hitler are beyond redemption," but he was convinced that "belief in nonviolence [is] based on the assumption that human nature in its essence is one and therefore unfailingly responds to the advances of love."[3] As it is evident, unlike Hitler or Stalin, Gandhi did not believe in the effectiveness of military power as a mode of national self-defence or as a realistic instrument in the process of nation-building. He explained his point of view on March 12, 1938, in the *Harijan*: "I am not enamoured by numbers," wrote Gandhi, "A peace army does not rely upon numbers, unless they understand the implications of nonviolence. I would, therefore, concentrate on a few becoming saturated with the spirit of nonviolence and disciplining themselves for the utmost suffering."[4] It is clear that Gandhi insists on the courage of conviction as a dynamic element of peacemaking. Keeping in mind his philosophy of nonviolent peace, this is how Gandhi believed that a *satyagrahi* should replace the logic of war by that of peace. For him, this was only possible by learning the "eternal law of suffering as the only remedy for undoing wrong and injustice."[5] Gandhi argued that only nonviolence could succeed against an opponent like Hitler, because it morally disarms the opponent by appealing to the sense of altruism of the other. However, the truth is that Gandhi was considered as a naïve idealist by any who were confronting Nazism during Second World War II. But for Gandhi, *ahimsa* was not the way of the coward; it was an art of fighting without fighting. As a result, he saw a true pacifist as a responsible *satyagrahi*. Gandhi even believed in the weapon of fasting against dictators. In an interview on April 28, 1939, he affirmed:

> I am fighting for peace, I shall die for peace, peace in the Congress, peace in the States, peace on earth, and goodwill amongst men. To set the seal upon that, if I feel the power, I am quite capable of fasting unto death to prevent Western humanity, which is getting ready to embark upon suicide on a scale hitherto unknown to the history of the world.[6]

Nine years later, on the eve of his death, Gandhi was asked to comment on his personal response to the atom bomb. He replied:

> I will not go underground. I will not go into shelter. I will come out in the open and let the pilot see I have not a trace evil against him. The pilot will not see our faces from his great height, I know. But that longing in our hearts – that he will not come to harm – would reach up to him and his eyes would be opened...If those thousands who were done to death in Hiroshima, if they had died with that prayerful action...died openly with that prayer in their hearts – their sacrifice would not have ended so disgracefully as it had.[7]

Gandhi insisted on several moral principles as the catalysts of his nonviolent resistance against wars and conflicts. The first principle advised by Gandhi to the *satyagrahis* was non-cooperation with the aggressor. The second was the preference of death to submission. The third and last principle was self-suffering. As such, we can admit that Gandhi had a very original way of looking at peace. Unlike many of us who consider peace as a state of happiness, Gandhi believed that peace would not take place without an effort of self-suffering. He underlined this opinion in a speech given at the Sabarmati Ashram during a prayer meeting on March 9, 1930, He asserted:

> The life of Rama, after the recovery of Sita, full of happiness as it was, does not occupy even a hundredth part of the epic. I want you all to treasure death and suffering more than life, and to appreciate their cleansing and purifying character.[8]

We need to understand that Gandhi did not envision self-suffering as a curse or an illness. He considered it as a form of moral courage and spiritual strength. According to him, this was part of every individual's self-discipline in preparing the world peace. Since the soldier of nonviolence did not use arms in order to struggle for peace, he/she had to use his/her soul force. In other words, Gandhi believed that every individual should purify himself/herself of violence through self-suffering. Gandhi identified himself with the sufferings of Others through self-suffering. He never fasted against an opponent, but in order to reform him/her. As he said, "I fasted to reform those who loved me."[9] Even here, Gandhi was in line with his altruistic and selfless ends. In fasting for peace, as for all other actions, Gandhi sought the help of what he described as his "inner voice." When asked on one occasion what he meant by Truth, he answered:

> What... is Truth? A difficult question; but I have solved it for myself by saying that it is what the voice within tells you. How then, you ask, different people think of different and contrary truths? Well, seeing that the human mind works through innumerable media and that the evolution of the human mind is not the same for all, it follows that what may be truth for one may be untruth for another, and hence those who have made

these experiments have come to the conclusion that there are certain conditions to be observed in making those experiments.... It is because we have at the present moment everybody claiming the right of conscience without going through any discipline whatsoever that there is so much untruth being delivered to a bewildered world. All that I can in true humility present to you is that Truth is not to be found by anybody who has not got an abundant sense of humility. If you would swim on the bosom of the ocean of Truth you must reduce yourself to a zero.[10]

Gandhi, actually, recognized that peacemaking, as an outward reconciliation, went hand in hand with an inward communion with oneself. This was also a process of accepting and manifesting openly and humbly one's frailty. "[We] think it is impossible to evoke the hidden powers of the soul," wrote Gandhi.

Well, I am engaged in trying to show, if I have any of these powers, that I am as frail a mortal as any of us and I never had anything extraordinary about me nor have any now. I claim to be a simple individual liable to err like any other fellow mortal.[11]

Unsurprisingly, Gandhi's quest for the otherness of the Others could also be considered as a methodology to prepare the individuals for peace with their opponents. As such, Gandhi's pedagogy for peace was a way to prepare world peace through interpersonal and intercommunal dialogue. This went hand in hand with the Gandhian philosophy of trusteeship, based on the sharing of wealth and economic equality. According to Thomas Weber, "the idea was to delegitimize the gross accumulation of wealth because in the final analysis, trusteeship is a 'principle of economic conscience'."[12] Trusteeship, like fasting, was considered for Gandhi as an effort of ethical self-balance. But, truly, Gandhi also saw peace as a form of trusteeship and a practice of altruism and selflessness at the global level. For Gandhi, the point was not to possess or to abolish anything but to gain with the Others. So, far from being a utopia, Gandhi's nonviolent path to world peace could be analysed as a practical way for the regeneration of a dialogical relationship between the communities around the globe. In the words of Humayun Kabir:

> Gandhi was a revolutionary who sought to transform human nature itself...Gandhi's answer to the problem of violence, internal or international, was to train a body of men and women who could have no internal tensions and would help to resolve tensions within society. Once tensions within society. Once tensions within society are reduced, international tensions will automatically diminish.[13]

Gandhi's pedagogy for peace was fully concentrated on universal empathy.

Gandhi knew well that empathy is the key to peacemaking and to the education of nonviolence in our world. What he suggested, therefore, was that cultures and traditions despite their differences of values could grasp an understanding of one another. As such, Gandhi maintained that all cultures despite their value-conflicts had a shared core of common humanity. For him, this common humanity was sufficient enough to enable mutual understanding and the possibility of peace among these diverse cultures. Accordingly, Gandhi's idea of a shared human horizon could have the critical force of avoiding moral anarchy and relativism while acknowledging the plurality of modes of being human. Therefore, Gandhi's empathetic pluralism was represented as more than simply an insight into the minds and lives of other humans. It was developed by Gandhi as a pedagogy to educate humanity against war and violence. Moreover, Gandhi's pedagogy for peace underlined the necessity for what we can call a "transformative education." Gandhi viewed peace education not only as an instrument in avoiding terror and violence but also as a way to self-realization and self-improvement. Thus, he placed a great emphasis on the cultural and moral aspects of peace education. According to Gandhi, peace education had to involve mutual interaction between means and ends, since nonviolence was analysed by him as the best means to understand the otherness of the Other. Therefore, for Gandhi peace and education had to be brought into a mutually interacting and empowering relation. Actually, pedagogy for peace was, for Gandhi, a critical attitude to all forms of ontological separateness and resentment which could end up with linguistic, psychological, cultural and political forms of violence. That is why, he pointed to two factors concerning the relation between education: peace and culture. The first factor was related to the cultural aspect of peace education. Regarding the role of culture in education, Gandhi affirms: "I attach for more importance to the cultural aspect of education than to the literary. Culture is the foundation, the primary thing."[14] When Gandhi talks about the importance of culture in education, he refers directly to the idea of building of character which prepares the moral life of an individual or a nation. This is why Gandhi rejected forcefully the utilitarian model of education, which maintained that economic or political ends justify teaching students the dominant economic or political models. Consequently, key to Gandhi's criticism of the utilitarian educational model was his awareness of the oneness of humanity and his belief in the importance of world peace. As a result, Gandhi's theory of Basic Education became one of the essential components of his pedagogy for peace. He, therefore, favoured the correlation between Basic Education and the idea of self-reliance and self-rule. He, therefore, made no distinction between intellectual and vocational training, because he considered peace education as a form of self-realization and self-transformation. Gandhi argued: "My [aim] is to change the very system of education. The new system will fulfil the needs of the country as well as the individual and bring about self-reliance. Self-reliance is also a true test of fulfillment of education."[15] Gandhi saw the way of peace through the capacity by all to regulate their lives. This was, according to him, a form of mental stability and moral growth. As he put it,

> The way of peace insures internal growth and stability. We reject it because we fancy that it involves submission to the will of the ruler who has imposed himself upon us...The suffering to be undergone...will be nothing

compared to the physical suffering and the moral loss we must incur in trying the way of war.[16]

Therefore, we can say that Gandhi's pedagogy of peace was a philosophy of becoming. Gandhi considered peace as what John Dewey referred to as a "moving idea." For Dewey, the business of the educator was to see that the ideas acquired by children and youth became moving ideas. Simply because moving ideas could help the individuals to become empathetic, responsive and self-reliant. So for Gandhi, the ultimate aim of peace education was to unfold diverse human experiences. This coincides further with the explicit Socratic nature of Gandhi's peace education and its teleological course towards bringing humanity to an awareness of its own moral aptitudes. By establishing a new task for peace education, Gandhi wanted to free humanity from its absolutist and calculative mode of thinking that nurtured wars and conflicts.

We can now understand why peace for Gandhi was not merely a distanced ideal but a duty. In Gandhi's philosophy of civilization, peacemaking was not just a process of self-proclamation of political harmony. For Gandhi, peacemaking was the ability to ensure that what a nation like India chose was the result of a sense of duty and understanding in regard to the other nations. This choice was not exercised as "obtaining peace from restraints" but as "obtaining peace through restraints." In the first formulation, peace was imposed by an "Other." In the second formulation, peace was a self-imposed situation. Therefore, peace is not only emancipation from war and conflict but also self-regulation of national and international relations through self-restraint. Hence, self-restraint forms an indispensable part of Gandhi's concept of peace. Therefore, true peace is a state of self-transcendence through self-restraint. As a result, peace is underlined by Gandhi as the reign of moral freedom. For Gandhi, peace was actually an experiment with truth. Gandhi's attempt in experimenting peace as a quest for truth was to hold to a universal value. Even if Gandhi was very loyal to India and to the Indian people, his responsibility as a universal peacemaker made him speak the truth beyond the national and the cultural frontiers by picking the right moral and political alternative and then intelligently representing it where it could do the best and cause the right change. In this respect, the contribution of Mahatma Gandhi in the cultivation of a public culture of peace, as an alternative to the system of conflict resolution put together by the states, is one of the most relevant issues which needs to be discussed today in political theory. Gandhi was very conscious about the fact that the cultivation of an ethics of peace requires the creation of institutions and practices, where the voice and perspective of everyone can be articulated and practised. In this respect, Gandhi is one of the main modern peace figures who had the disturbing capacity to shake our inherited conceptual habit about peacemaking and to let us see peace in a new light. Gandhi proclaimed:

> The science of war leads one to dictatorship pure and simple. The science of nonviolence alone can lead on to pure democracy...[Dictators] have up to now always found ready response to the violence they have used. Within their experience, they have not come across organized nonviolent resistance on an appreciable scale, if at all. Therefore, it is not only highly unlikely, but... inevitable, that they would recognize the superiority of nonviolent resistance over any display of violence that they may be capable of putting forth.[17]

As we all are aware, for Gandhi, peace is a creed, a matter of principle and not merely a technique for conflict resolution. It is a principle to which the states and the citizens must be committed. As such, the concept of "enemy" is absent in Gandhi's social and political vocabulary. If Gandhi ever had any enemies in life, they were no others than anger and pride. He once said:

> It is no easy thing to walk on the sharp sword-edge of ahimsa in this world which is full of himsa. Wealth does not help; anger is the enemy of ahimsa; and pride is a monster that swallows it up. In this strait and narrow observance of this religion of ahimsa one has often to know so-called himsa as the truest form of ahimsa.[18]

According to Gandhi, a *satyagrahi* should always overcome pride, anger, lust and greed. As a result, Gandhi had a different approach of offence and defence in time of war. He argued:

> I see no bravery nor sacrifice in destroying life or property for offence or defence... There is reason, *sacrifice* and even *bravery* in so leaving my homestead and crops, if I do so *not* out of fear but because I refuse to regard anyone as my enemy...[19]

It would be a mistake to assume that by not having enemies, Gandhi was completely alienated from the realities of war and peace. On the contrary, Gandhi recognized the extreme situations of life such as wars, epidemics or revolutions but always maintained nonviolence as the nobler and humanitarian way. This remark emphasizes the point previously made on the idea of "maturity" in the Gandhian philosophy of peace. It is interesting that though Gandhi never was a reader of Immanuel Kant, he is very close to the Kantian idea of "maturity" developed in his famous essay "*Was ist Aufklärung?*." Nearly, 240 years ago, in 1784, Kant responded to the question posed by a Berlin newspaper, "What is Enlightenment?," by equating Enlightenment with the attainment of maturity through the use of reason. Kant answers the question in the first sentence of the essay: "Enlightenment is man's emergence from his self-incurred immaturity."[20] It would not be wrong to affirm that Gandhi also believed that "maturity" consists in humans taking over responsibility for their actions by using critical rationality. For Gandhi, critical rationality consisted in the unflinching examination of our most cherished and confronting assumptions. He called it the "acid test of reason." In 1925, Gandhi wrote:

> Every formula of every religion has, in this age of reason, to submit to the acid test of reason and universal justice if it is to ask for universal assent. Error can claim no exemption even if it can be supported by the scriptures of the world.[21]

What emerges from this quote is that Gandhi recognized the weakness of an appeal to peace alone based on supposed spiritual or political authority. He knew well that peace-seeking and peacemaking should be strengthened by the work of citizens as mature spirits. Gandhi was in fact a stern defender of individual autonomy next to the idea of citizen's moral duty. But in no way did Gandhi support any form of fanaticism, either religious or rationalist. Knowing the limits of reason, Gandhi points out to the possible lunatic nature of it. He warns, "Just as matter misplaced becomes dirt, reason misused becomes lunacy."[22] In due course, Gandhi did not admit that reason is an exclusive determinant of a mature and responsible process of peacemaking. He believed also in the work of the heart. As he underlined to the Quakers in Birmingham on October 18, 1931:

> Nobody has probably drawn up more petitions or espoused more forlorn causes than I, and I have come to this fundamental conclusion that, if you want something really important to be done, you must not merely satisfy the reason, you must move the heart also. The appeal of reason is more to the head, but the penetration of the heart comes from suffering. It opens up the inner understanding in man. Suffering is the badge of the human race, not the sword.[23]

Gandhi knew well that critical reasoning is necessary for peacemaking, but not sufficient. He believed that a *satyagrahi* needed to strengthen his/her reason by an act of suffering. As we said previously, Gandhi considered suffering as a moral act. Therefore, he saw a work of compassion, in addition to that of reason. Humans suffered for the Other and understood the suffering of the Other, because they were indebted to the world. As such, Gandhi also explained peace as a form of indebtedness to the world. As mentioned earlier, for Gandhi, peace had a spiritual content which remained largely agnostic. It went in the direction of Gandhi's idea of self-realization as an experience of self-transformation. As explained before, Gandhi stressed this ability to self-transformation as a collective capacity to live in harmony. Therefore, what Gandhi aspired to achieve was a self-ruled peace or a grassroots process of peacemaking. Gandhi envisioned such a situation as a state of peace without political power. It goes without saying that in Gandhi's political philosophy, the ideal peace and the ideal society went hand in hand. He described his ideal society as a collective space where

> representatives will become unnecessary if the national life becomes so perfect as to be self-controlled. It will then be a state of enlightened anarchy in which each person will become his own ruler. He will conduct himself in such a way that his behaviour will not hamper the well-being of his neighbours. In an ideal State there will be no political institution and therefore no political power.[24]

As we can see, Gandhi's pedagogy for peace was closely related with his vision of democracy. For Gandhi, democracy was an institution not only of rights but also of equities and opportunities. He defined democracy in the following terms: "My notion of democracy is that under it the weakest should have the same opportunity as the strongest. That can never happen except through non-violence."[25] As a result, Gandhi envisioned democracy as an ethical solution to the problems of the Indian society and the world, and not just as a political regime. That is why he argued that the path of democratic governance should be achieved through the ethical imperatives of nonviolence. As such, Gandhi saw a close relationship between synthesis between the inclusive principles of nonviolence and the practical realization of an egalitarian democracy. Consequently, he believed that only nonviolence could translate a liberal democracy into pluralistic and egalitarian mode of social life. Evidently, for Gandhi democracy could only function with the existence of a responsible citizenry. "Most people do not understand the complicated machinery of the government," he observed.

> They do not realize that every citizen silently but none the less certainly sustains the government of the day in

ways of which he has no knowledge. Every citizen therefore renders himself responsible for every act of his government. And it is quite proper to support it so long as the actions of the government are bearable. But when they hurt him and his nation, it becomes his duty to withdraw his support.[26]

This is where Gandhi's conception of democracy becomes relevant and significant to contemporary peace theory. Gandhi had come to the conclusion that democracy, like any other aspect of social and political life, would not function in the framework of a violent civilization of wars and conflicts, with no sense of ethics. Therefore, as in his theory of peace, Gandhi joined the personal and the political in his theory of democracy. According to him, a self-governed democracy had for goal a self-governed peace. Moreover, both peace and democracy were the outcomes of civic awareness. Gandhi described this process in the following words:

> Self-government depends entirely upon our internal strength, upon our ability to fight against the heaviest odds. Indeed, self-government which does not require that continuous striving to attain it and to sustain it is not worth the name. I have, therefore, endeavoured to show both in the word and deed, that, political self-government, that is, Self-government for a large number of men and women, is no better than individual self-government, and therefore, it is to be attained by precisely the same means that are required for individual self-government or self-rule.[27]

It is against such a backdrop that the status and value of peace in Gandhi's writings and his attitudes towards the two world wars in the 20th century need to be understood. Gandhi, as an individual, but also as a mass leader, understood that he needed to be judged as a peacemaker and not just as a politician. He said, "To understand what I say one needs to understand my conduct."[28] Even if some concepts, such as power or government, might fail to explain the ethical and spiritual essence of Gandhi's struggle, peace is certainly not one of them. Gandhi's strategy for peace remained dependent on the exemplarity of individuals and nations. Assuredly, this was a difficult task, with some obvious and serious limitations and weaknesses, especially during the war time. But, Gandhi's vision of world peace went beyond the Indian struggle for independence. It was a vision of a new world and a contribution to the future destiny of humanity.

Notes

1 Panter-Brick, Simone, *Gandhi and Nationalism*, op. cit., p. 72.
2 Chandhoke, Neera, "Negating Violence: The Gandhi Way", in Pfost, Eva (ed.) *Between Ethics and Politics: Gandhi Today*, Routledge, New Delhi, 2014, p. 82.
3 Gandhi, Mahatma, *For Pacifists*, Navajivan, Ahmedabad, 1949, p. 79.
4 Gandhi, Mahatma, *Collected Works of Mahatma Gandhi*, op. cit., vol. 66, 1976, p. 398.
5 Ibid., p. 398.
6 Ibid., vol. 69, p. 178.
7 Quoted in Gangal, S.C., *The Gandhian Way to World Peace*, Vora&Co. Publishers, Bombay, 1960, pp. 63–64.
8 Gandhi, Mahatma, *Collected Works of Mahatma Gandhi*, op. cit., vol. 43, 1971, pp. 30–31.
9 Fischer, Louis, *The Essential Gandhi*, op. cit., p. 210.
10 Gandhi, Mahatma, *All Men Are Brothers*, op. cit., p. 120.
11 Fischer, Louis, *The Essential Gandhi*, op. cit., p. 206.
12 Weber, Thomas, "Gandhi's Moral Economics", in Parel, Anthony & Brown, Judith M. (ed.) *The Cambridge Companion to Gandhi*, Cambridge University Press, New Delhi, 2011, p. 143.
13 Kabir, Humayun, "Gandhi's Revolutionary Significance", in Radakrishnan, S. (ed.) Mahatma *Gandhi 100 Years*, Gandhi Peace Foundation, New Delhi, 1968, pp. 186–187.
14 Gandhi, Mahatma, Harijan, May 5, 1946.
15 Gandhi, Mahatma, *Collected Works of Mahatma Gandhi*, op. cit., vol. 70, p. 277.
16 Fischer, Louis, op. cit., p. 202.
17 Ibid., pp. 333–334.
18 Gandhi, Mahatma, *Young India*, October 21, 1926.
19 Fischer, Louis, op. cit., p. 332.
20 Kant, Immanuel, *An Answer to the Question: What Is Enlightenment?* Great Ideas, Penguin Books, London, 2009, p. 1.

21 Gandhi, Mahatma, "Young India", February 26, 1925, in *The Collected Works of Mahatma Gandhi*, Volume 26, p. 202.
22 Ibid., October 14, 1926, vol. 31, p. 496.
23 Ibid., November 5, 1931, vol. 48, p. 189.
24 Gandhi, Mahatma, January 1939, in *The Collected Works of Mahatma Gandhi*, Volume 68, p. 265.
25 Gandhi, Mahatma, *All Men Are Brothers*, op. cit., p. 1217.
26 Ibid., p. 228.
27 Gandhi, Mahatma, *Young India*, December 1, 1927.
28 Gandhi, Mahatma, "Letter to Hanumanprasad Poddar", quoted in Kolge, Nishikant, *Gandhi against Caste*, Oxford University Press, New Delhi, 2017, p. 6.

4

GANDHI AND THE STRUGGLE FOR PEACE

"A votary of Ahimsa [Nonviolence]," wrote Gandhi,

> remains true to his faith if the spring of all his actions is compassion...When two nations are fighting, the duty of a votary of Ahimsa is to stop the war. He who is not equal to that duty, he who has no power of resisting war, he who is not qualified to resist war may take part in war and yet whole- heartedly try to free himself, his nation and the world from war.[1]

Gandhi's appreciation of war and peace was linked to his challenge of concentrated power and his search to empower the powerless. Yet, his confrontations with the harsh realities of the two world wars in the 20th century were always based on his willingness to act on behalf of the victims. From Gandhi's perspective, wars and conflicts robbed their victims from their free will and made them complacent. Therefore, for Gandhi, making autonomous decisions in times of war was more important than anything else. According to Gandhi, the British triumphed in India not because they were modern but because of the moral weakness of Indians. In that sense, Gandhi was probably the first modern Indian political thinker to think of war and peace not in terms of strength and weakness but in terms of moral dignity and self-respect drawn on the civilizational resources of a spiritual society like India. In that sense, Gandhi produced the most effective ethical response to the worldview of modern warfare by drawing notably on the civilizational resources of Hindu tradition. As Francis G. Hutchins explains in his book *Gandhi's Battlefield Choice*,

> Gandhi invoked in a new way the *Bhagavad Gita*'s exhortation to stand and fight as a last resort, even against foes one respects...He argued that in modern times the war depicted in the two-thousand-year old *Gita* could be most productively thought of as a contest within every human being between good and evil impulses.[2]

Gandhi drew different lessons from the *Gita* in his different encounters and confrontations with the British.

> Gandhi's own role as a political leader had meanwhile also evolved. During World War I, Gandhi had loyally helped recruit Indian soldiers to fight for the British Empire in distant lands, only to see the British then renege on their promises to reward India's war services with greater political autonomy.[3]

Mohandas Gandhi was in South Africa when the Great War broke out in 1914. A year later he returned to India and advised his friends and colleagues to suspend their struggle against the British and help them in their war efforts against Germany. In April 1918, Gandhi was called to the War Conference by the viceroy, where he supported the recruitment for war. Though he preferred to speak in Hindustani, he was well aware of expressing a gesture of empathy towards the Empire. In addition to his short speech at the conference, Gandhi wrote a letter to the viceroy, re-affirming his good will to help the British. He wrote:

> If I could make my countrymen retrace their steps, I would make them withdraw all the Congress resolutions, and not whisper "Home Rule" or "Responsible Government" during the pendency of the war. I would make India offer all her able-bodied sons as a sacrifice to the Empire at its critical moment; and I know that India

> by this very act would become the most favoured partner in the Empire and racial distinctions would become a thing of the past... Whilst, therefore, it is clear to me that we should give to the Empire every available man for its defence. I fear that I cannot say the same thing about financial assistance. My intimate intercourse with the [riots] convinces me that India has already donated to the Imperial Exchequer beyond her capacity. I know that, in making this statement, I am voicing the opinion of the vast majority of my countrymen. I write this, because I love the English Nation, and I wish to evoke in every Indian the loyalty of the Englishman.[4]

One of the significant points in Gandhi's letter is his transparent conviction that one could extend the goodness of human nature to the opponents. In fact, Gandhi deeply believed that peacemaking would not be possible without the transcendence of selfish national interests. Of course, this was a big trial for him, because he had to support the virtues of nonviolence while recruiting soldiers for the war.

> Some of Gandhi's ashram colleagues told him (as Polak had done earlier) that recruiting soldier did not seem like ahimsa to them. Gandhi's reply was that an Indian's ahimsa was often a mask for cowardice...Discipline – even military discipline – would be a step towards true nonviolence and yield the strength with which "we may even fight the Empire should it play foul with us". National interest was clashing with nonviolence in his mind, yet the ethical dilemma too was real.[5]

As mentioned previously, Gandhi considered the problem of peace as an ethical issue rather than as a political one. For him, the importance was to be on the side of the right and the just. He explained more on this subject in a letter that he published in *Harijan* on December 9, 1939. He observed:

> The moral influence would be used on the side of peace. I have already said in these columns that my nonviolence

does recognize different species of violence – defensive and offensive. It is true that in the long run the difference is obliterated, but the initial merit persists. A nonviolent person is bound, when the occasion arises, to say which side is just. Thus, I wished success to the Abyssinians, the Spaniards, the Czechs, the Chinese and the Poles, though in each case I wished that they could have offered nonviolent resistance... But who am I? I have no strength save what God gives me. I have no authority over my countrymen save the purely moral. If God holds me to be a pure instrument for the spread of nonviolence in the place of the awful violence now ruling the earth, He will give me the strength and show me the way. My greatest weapon is mute prayer.[6]

This letter by Gandhi explains a great deal on his psychology as a moral leader in time of war. It also shows clearly that Gandhi was a man of peace, who beyond the violent values of his time, could struggle for peace, nonviolence and dialogue among nations. Based on this assumption, it appears that the most appropriate way to interpret Gandhi's approval of violence against cowardice is to consider him as a consistent thinker on the issue of peace. Hence, it would be wrong to say that there were gradual changes in Gandhi's opinions on war and peace. If it is accepted that Gandhi always had a peace strategy even when he wrote on violence against cowardice, then we can establish a continuity between his writings on war and peace in different stages of his struggle. Gandhi wrote:

> I do believe that where there is only a choice between cowardice and violence I would advise violence. Thus when my eldest son asked me what he should have done, had he been present when I was almost fatally assaulted in 1908, whether he should have run away and seen me killed or whether he should have used his physical force which he could and wanted to use, and defended me, I told him that it was his duty to defend me even by using violence. Hence it was that I took part in the Boer War, the so called Zulu rebellion and [World War I]. Hence

also do I advocate training in arms for those who believe in the method of violence. I would rather have India resort to arms in order to defend her honor than that she should in a cowardly manner become or remain a helpless witness to her own dishonor. But I believe that nonviolence is infinitely superior to violence, forgiveness is more manly than punishment... But... forgiveness only when there is the power to punish.... A mouse hardly forgives a cat when it allows itself to be torn to pieces by her. I therefore appreciate the sentiment of those who cry out for the condign punishment of General Dyer and his ilk. They would tear him to pieces if they could. But I do not believe myself to be a helpless creature. Only I want to use India's and my strength for better purpose.[7]

Gandhi's observation on the choice of violence against cowardice was in no way an abandonment of his fundamental commitment to nonviolence. This said, Gandhi certainly never dissociated nonviolence and violence, either in reality or as major concepts of his political philosophy. Therefore, we can understand his position when he affirmed that an action "may wear the appearance of violence" and yet be "absolutely nonviolent in the highest sense."[8]

Gandhi compared World War I to the battle of the Mahabharata, with all its miseries and ruins. Yet, Gandhi remained loyal to the Empire during World War I. However, "when World War II began in 1939, neither Gandhi personally nor most Indians could any longer imagine that loyalty to the Empire would lead to freedom for India."[9] Gandhi was fully aware of the circumstances that eventually led up to World War II. His opinion on the 1928 Kellogg-Briand Pact was that it was simply a shrewd tactic to carry on the joint exploitation peacefully, to preserve the status quo, to continue the arms race and to prepare for a deadlier war than World War I. In 1935, Mussolini's attack on Abyssinia tragically confirmed Gandhi's suspicions. In a cabled message to *The Cosmopolitan*, he wrote:

> If recognised leaders of mankind who have control over the engines of destruction were wholly to renounce their

use with full knowledge of the implications, permanent peace can be obtained. This is clearly impossible without the great powers of the earth renouncing their imperialistic designs. This again seems impossible without these great nations ceasing to believe in soul-destroying competition and the desire to multiply wants and therefore increase their material possessions.[10]

Gandhi advised the Abyssinians not to make appeal to the League of Nations, rather he called them to resort to nonviolence and non-cooperation to defeat Mussolini. On a different note, Gandhi was also concerned about Japan's aggression against China and constantly maintained that no matter what, China should respond to the aggression in a nonviolent way. He urged Chinese people not to take up arms against the Japanese, because he believed that a victory through violence "would not bring a new hope for the world."[11]

The main concern of Gandhi during World War II were the Jews. Gandhi radically rejected the Nazi persecution of the Jews. But in this case, he maintained that if at all any war was justified, it would be a war against Germany for all the brutalities committed by Adolf Hitler, which are unparalleled in the history of humanity. In an article published in 1938, Gandhi bitterly admitted:

> If there ever could be a justifiable war in the name of and for humanity, a war against Germany, to prevent the wanton persecution of a whole race, would be completely justified. But I do not believe in any war. A discussion of the pros and cons of such a war is, therefore, outside my horizon or province[12]

Gandhi wanted the world powers to stop this madness before it was too late, but they, at that point, were more inclined towards appeasing Hitler. Gandhi argued:

> If I have called the arrangement with Herr Hitler "peace without honour", it was not to cast any reflection

> on British or French statesmen. I have no doubt that Mr. Chamberlain could not think of anything better. He knew his nation's limitations. He wanted to avoid war, if it could be avoided at all. Short of going to war, he pulled his full weight in favour of the Czechs. That it could not save honour was no fault of his. It would be so every time there is a struggle with Herr Hitler or Signor Mussolini. It cannot be otherwise. Democracy dreads to spill blood. The philosophy for which the two dictators' stand calls it cowardice to shrink from carnage. They exhaust the resources of poetic art in order to glorify organized murder. There is no humbug about their word or deed. They are ever ready for war. There is nobody in Germany or Italy to cross their path. Their word is law.[13]

Nevertheless, while Gandhi was asking the Allied forces to stop Hitler, he reminded Jews that these outside sympathies would not help their cause and they had to offer *Satyagraha* to Hitler to win this fight. Mahatma Gandhi had no illusion about the Munich Pact, signed between Britain and France, on the one hand, and Germany, on the other, in October 1938. For him, the Pact was "peace without honor" and a big failure on the part of Britain and France to stop the war from happening. Gandhi was also worried for the less powerful countries which were getting exploited and were at the danger of getting absorbed by the more powerful ones. After the betrayal of Czechoslovakia by Britain and France, as the result of the signed Munich Pact, Gandhi wrote to Hitler on July 23, 1939, pleading for the preservation of peace in the world. Gandhi wrote:

> Friends have been urging me to write to you for the sake of humanity. But I have resisted their request, because of the feeling that any letter from me would be an impertinence. Something tells me that I must not calculate and that I must make my appeal for whatever it may be worth. It is quite clear that you are today the one person in the world who can prevent a war which may reduce humanity to the savage state. Must you pay the price for

an object however worthy it may appear to you to be? Will you listen to the appeal of one who has deliberately [sic] shunned the method of war not without considerable success? Any way I anticipate your forgiveness, if I have erred in writing to you.[14]

A month later the world was plunged into a terrible war. Hitler invaded Poland in September 1939. Britain and France had immediately declared war on Germany, thus putting the start to World War II. The Governor and Viceroy of India, Lord Victor A. Linlithgow, without consulting the representative opinion of Indian leaders, committed the country to the war. The Indian leadership felt humiliated.

But returning to Gandhi's letter to Hitler, it should be noted that, despite the fact that Gandhi was a convinced anti-colonialist, he never made the mistake of justifying Nazism or Fascism. He firmly believed that these ideologies are violent, non-compassionate and a great threat to the principles of democracy. However, earlier, in 1921, Gandhi had made it clear, through the columns of *Young India*, that even the threat of being imprisoned or sent to the gallows would not persuade him to participate in the wars of Britain, or for the matter of that, in any other war. In fact, Gandhi held Britain and France directly responsible for the rise of Nazism. He considered the Versailles Treaty as a treaty of revenge, and Hitler, Mussolini and Stalin as leaders who "are able to show the immediate effectiveness of violence."[15] Further Gandhi bitterly noted, "The democracies therefore that we see at work in England, America and France are only so-called, because they are no less based on violence than Nazi Germany, Fascist Italy or even Soviet Russia."[16] It is evident that Gandhi had genuine concerns about world peace and felt that India had the potential to contribute in that regard. At the same time he understood that "for India – a big nation – to be not able to help, although it is conscious that it can render inestimable help in a variety of ways that it would ensure victory for Allies,"[17] Gandhi emphasized that India need to be independent in order to help the Allied forces and never believed that World War II, or any war, could bring in a decisive victory for anyone. He observed: "If some country resorts to methods which I consider to be inhuman, I may not follow them."[18]

As someone who was fully devoted to peace and nonviolence, Gandhi was the supporter of both the Muslims and the Jews in the two world wars. His collaboration with the Khilafat movement in India was more than a strategy to build the solidarity among the Hindus and the Muslims against His Majesty's government. Gandhi's involvement with the fierce believers in a pan-Islamic movement "was essentially a natural progression from the status he had prized in South Africa as spokesman for Muslim grievances, and from his championship of the Ali brothers during the war."[19] Gandhi expressed his sympathy for the Muslims and the Khilafat movement at the Delhi Imperial War Conference in 1918 and later followed it up by a letter to the Viceroy, Lord Chelmsford. "As a Hindu," he mentioned in the letter, "I cannot be indifferent to their cause. Their sorrows must be our sorrows."[20] Certainly, Gandhi's deliberate attachment to the Muslims and the Khilafat movement helped him in reaching a new vision of peace for India and the world. Though the Khilafat movement was not a great success story, Gandhi, however, remained close to some Muslims leaders, like Maulana Azad or Khan Abdul Ghaffar Khan, until the time of his assassination. Gandhi shared a vision of a nonviolent and peacemaking Islam with Ghaffar Khan, which included a strategy of reconciliation between India and Pakistan.

Undoubtedly, it was through the Khilafat question that Gandhi became indirectly involved with the problems of Jews and Muslims in Palestine. During his involvement with the Khilafat movement, Gandhi's position on the question of Palestine was clearly in favour of the Muslims. As he declared in March 1921 to the *Bombay Chronicle*:

> The existence of Islam demands the total abrogation of mandates taken by Britain and France. No influence, direct or indirect, over the Holy Places of Islam will ever be tolerated by Indian Muslims. It follows, therefore, that even Palestine must be under Muslim control. So far as I am aware, there never has been any difficulty put

in the way of Jews and Christians visiting Palestine and performing all their religious rites. No canon, however, of ethics or war can possibly justify the gift by the Allies of Palestine to Jews.[21]

Assuredly, Mahatma Gandhi, unlike Mohammed Ali Jinnah and the Muslim League, did not have a clear-cut agenda for the Muslims in Palestine, but it took him ten more years to empathize with the Jewish claims on Palestine. It was during his visit to London in 1931 to attend the Round Table Conference that he spoke out on Zionism. In response to a question from *The Jewish Chronicle* on October 2, 1931, Gandhi proclaimed:

> I have a world of friends among the Jews ... (They should) realize the Jerusalem that is within. Zionism meaning reoccupation of Palestine has no attraction for me. I can understand the longing of a Jew to return to Palestine, and he can do so if he can without the help of bayonets, whether his own or those of Britain. In that event he would go to Palestine peacefully and in perfect friendliness with the Arabs. The real Zionism of which I have given you my meaning is the thing to strive for, long for, and die for. Zion lies in one's heart. It is the abode of God. The real Jerusalem is the spiritual Jerusalem. Thus he can realize Zionism in any part of the world.[22]

It would be fair to say that Gandhi was not directly interested with the Muslim or Jewish problems in Palestine outside the context of the Indian independence. However, as it is put forward by Simone Panter-Brick, Gandhi

> was drawn into the affairs of Palestine, in two ways that tended to be contradictory. In the first phase that covered the years 1919 to 1924, he acted as a convinced pro-Arab agitator. In the next, he showed pro-Jewish sympathy and tried to act on it. Circumstances had changed. Palestine was now a nation and the economy

was booming. Jews made up a third of its population instead of a tenth. The Mandatory power could not cope satisfactorily with the implementation of the Balfour Declaration. Gandhi wanted to help the Jews, but the animosity of the Muslim League, led by Jinnah, paralysed his initiatives.[23]

With the rise of Nazism in Germany and the politics of de-judification of Europe by the Nazis, Gandhi had a new approach to the question of Jewish survival and its significance for the world peace. In an article in the *Harijan* of November 11, 1938, "Gandhi condemned 'the German persecution of the Jews' as having 'no parallel in history' and warned that 'The calculated violence of Hitler may even result in a general massacre of the Jews.'"[24] As we can see, Gandhi reacted to the Nazi persecution of the Jews before the start of the war, but the solutions that he had offered based on his principles of nonviolent resistance were far from being accepted as "realistic" by many German Jews. Gandhi argued:

> Germany is showing to the world how efficiently violence can be worked when it is not hampered by any hypocrisy or weakness masquerading as humanitarianism. It is also showing how hideous, terrible and terrifying it looks in its nakedness. Can the Jews resist this organized and shameless persecution? Is there a way to preserve their self-respect, and not to feel helpless, neglected and forlorn? I submit there is...If I were a Jew and were born in Germany and earned my livelihood there, I would claim Germany as my home even as the tallest gentile German might, and challenge him to shoot me or cast me in the dungeon; I would refuse to be expelled or to submit to discriminating treatment. And for doing this I should not wait for the fellow Jews to join me in civil resistance, but would have confidence that in the end the rest were bound to follow my example. If one Jew or all the Jews were to accept the prescription here offered, he or they cannot be worse off than now.[25]

GANDHI AND THE STRUGGLE FOR PEACE

Gandhi's open letter to the German Jews, advocating nonviolent resistance against the Nazi aggression, was intended to prevent World War II. However, by doing so, Gandhi was plunging into dangerous waters. The critics were not long in coming. The most famous one was from Martin Buber, a Jewish philosopher, newly arrived in Palestine. In a letter to Gandhi, written on February 24, 1939, Buber criticized Gandhi for making a comparison between the persecution of Jews in Germany and Indians in South Africa at the time of the *Satyagraha* campaign. Buber wrote:

> Jews are being persecuted, robbed, maltreated, tortured, murdered. And you, Mahatma Gandhi, say that their position in the country where they suffer all this is an exact parallel to the position of Indians in South Africa at the time you inaugurated your famous "Force of Truth" or "Strength of the Soul" (Satyagraha) campaign. There the Indians occupied precisely the same place, and the persecution there also had a religious tinge. There also the constitution denied equality of rights to the white and the black race including the Asiatics; there also the Indians were assigned to ghettos, and the other disqualifications were, at all events, almost of the same type as those of the Jews in Germany. I read and re-read these sentences in your article without being able to understand. Although I know them well, I re-read your South African speeches and writings, and called to mind, with all the attention and imagination at my command, every complaint you made therein, and I did likewise with the accounts of your friends and pupils at that time. But all this did not help me to understand what you say about us. In the first of your speeches with which I am acquainted, that of 1896, you quoted two particular incidents to the accompaniment of hisses from your audience: first, that a band of Europeans had set fire to an Indian village shop, causing some damage; and, second, that another band had thrown burning rockets into an urban shop. If I oppose to this the thousands and thousands of Jewish shops destroyed and burned out, you will perhaps

answer that the difference is only one of quantity and
that the proceedings were of almost the same type. But,
Mahatma, are you not aware of the burning of syna-
gogues and scrolls of the Law? Do you know nothing of
all the sacred property of the community – some of it of
great antiquity – that has been destroyed in the flames?
I am not aware that Boers and Englishmen in South
Africa ever injured anything sacred to the Indians. I find
only one other concrete complaint quoted in that speech,
namely, that three Indian schoolteachers, who were
found walking in the streets after 9.00 p.m. contrary to
orders, were arrested and only acquitted later on. That
is the only incident of the kind you bring forward. Now
do you know or do you not know, Mahatma, what a
concentration camp is like and what goes on there? Do
you know of the torments in the concentration camp,
of its methods of slow and quick slaughter? I cannot assume that you know of this; for then this tragi-comic
utterance "of almost the same type" could scarcely have
crossed your lips. Indians were despised and despicably
treated in South Africa. But they were not deprived of
rights, they were not outlawed, they were not hostages to
a hoped-for change in the behaviour of foreign Powers.
And do you think perhaps that a Jew in Germany could
pronounce in public one single sentence of a speech such
as yours without being knocked down? Of what significance is it to point to a certain something in common
when such differences are overlooked?[26]

From reading Buber's letter to Gandhi, we can understand his
anger due to Gandhi's misunderstanding of the Jewish persecution in Germany. But Buber was also concerned with Gandhi's
misreading of the Jewish claim to Palestine. He underlined:

You, Mahatma Gandhi, who know of the connexion between tradition and future, should not associate yourself
with those who pass over our cause without understanding or sympathy. But you say – and I consider it to be

the most significant of all the things you tell us – that Palestine belongs to the Arabs and that it is therefore "wrong and inhuman to impose the Jews on the Arabs". Here I must add a personal note in order to make clear to you on what premises I desire to consider this matter. I belong to a group of people who, from the time when Britain conquered Palestine, have not ceased to strive for the achievement of genuine peace between Jew and Arab. By genuine peace, we inferred and still infer that both peoples should together develop the Land without one imposing his will on the other. In view of the international usages of our generation, this appeared to us to be very difficult but not impossible. We were and still are well aware that in this unusual – even unexampled – case, it is a question of seeking new ways of understanding and cordial agreement between the nations. Here again, we stood and still stand under the sway of a commandment. We considered it a fundamental point that in this case two vital claims are opposed to each other, two claims of a different nature and a different origin, which cannot be pitted one against the other and between which no objective decision can be made as to which is just or unjust. We considered and still consider it our duty to understand and to honour the claim that is opposed to ours and to endeavour to reconcile both claims. We cannot renounce the Jewish claim; something even higher than the life of our people is bound up with the Land, namely, the work that is their divine mission. But we have been and still are convinced that it must be possible to find some form of agreement between this claim and the other; for we love this land and we believe in its future, and, seeing that such love and such faith are surely present on the other side as well, a union in the common service of the Land must be within the range of the possible. Where there is faith and love, a solution may be found even to what appears to be a tragic contradiction.[27]

Gandhi never responded to Buber. The reason is not clear. Most probably, as Simone Panther-Brik suggests, because he "was tired of the controversy around his article."[28] In any event, in the past 70 years, many famous critics of Gandhi's nonviolence have pointed their fingers at this controversy or simply at the impotence of Gandhian nonviolence against totalitarian regimes like Nazism. Among these, the most famous one comes from Hannah Arendt, who mentioned Gandhi only once in her writings, and that was in her essay "On Violence," where she underlines, "If Gandhi's enormously powerful and successful strategy of nonviolent resistance had met with a different enemy – Stalin's Russia, Hitler's Germany, even prewar Japan, instead of England, the outcome would not have been decolonization, but massacre and submission."[29] However, unlike Arendt, who was interested in the work of the political in the public realm as a stage for speech and action, Gandhi believed that in the absence of a concrete ethical foundation, the political could not function democratically and nonviolently. Therefore, for Gandhi, the essential task of the political was to bring moral progress to human community. The major contrast between Gandhi and Hitler was that the latter believed in eliminating *morality* from *politics*. Whereas for Mahatma Gandhi, the most important was the moral legitimacy of nonviolence as a strategy of peacemaking. That is why Gandhi is impossible to classify in terms of conventional categories of peace studies and conflict resolution. Gandhi remains an original thinker in matter of peacebuilding and also an astute peacebuilder who was willing to learn from other nations.

Notes

1 Fischer, Louis, *The Essential Gandhi*, op. cit., p. 125.
2 Hutchins, Francis G., *Gandhi's Battlefield Choice: The Mahatma, The Bhagavad Gita and World War II*, Manohar, New Delhi, 2017, pp. 8–9.
3 Ibid., p. 9.
4 Gandhi, Mahatma, *The Collected Works of Mahatma Gandhi*, op. cit., vol. 14, pp. 378–380.
5 Gandhi, Rajmohan, *Mohandas: A True Story of a Man, His People and an Empire*, Penguin –Viking, New Delhi, 2006, p. 214.
6 Gandhi, Mahatma, *The Collected Works of Mahatma Gandhi*, op. cit., vol. 71, pp. 10–11.

7 Fischer, Louis, op. cit., pp. 156–157.
8 Bose, Nirmal Kumar (ed.), *Selections from Gandhi*, Navajivan Publishing, Ahmedabad, 1968, p. 177.
9 Hutchins, Francis G., *Gandhi's Battlefield Choice: The Mahatma, The Bhagavad Gita and World War II*, Manohar, New Delhi, 2017, p. 65.
10 Quoted in Puri, R.S., "Gandhi and the Second World War." *The Indian Journal of Political Science*, 38 (1), 1977, pp. 30–53.
11 Bondurant, J. (ed.), *Harijan: Collected Issues of Gandhi's Journals, 1933–1955*, 19 Volumes, Garland Publishing, New York, Volume III, 1973, p. 443.
12 Gandhi, Mahatma, *The Collected Works of Mahatma Gandhi*, op. cit., vol. 74, p. 240.
13 Gandhi, Mahatma, *Harijan*, October 15, 1938.
14 Gandhi, Mahatma, "Letter to Adolf Hitler," quoted in *The Observer*, Saturday October 12, 2013.
15 Fischer, Louis, op. cit., p. 331.
16 Quoted in Ashu Pasricha, Ashu & Misra, R.P., *Rediscovering Gandhi*, Volume 4, Consensual Democracy: Gandhi on State Power and Politics Concept Publishing Company, New Delhi, 2010, p. 84.
17 Tendulkar, D.G., *Mahatma; Life of Mohandas Karamchand Gandhi*, Ministry of Information and Broadcasting Government of India, New Delhi, 1961 (1951), p. 171.
18 Fischer, Louis, op. cit., p. 332.
19 Brown, Judith M., *Gandhi: Prisoner of Hope*, Yale University Press, New Haven, CT, 1989, p. 140.
20 Gandhi to Chelmsford, April 29, 1918, in *The Collected Works of Mahatma Gandhi*, op. cit., vol. 14, p. 377.
21 Gandhi, Mahatma, *The Collected Works of Mahatma Gandhi*, op. cit., vol. 19, p. 444.
22 Ibid., vol. 48, p. 106.
23 Panter-Brick, Simone, "Palestine, the Caliph and Gandhi: A Nonviolent Jihad", in *Asian Social Science*, Volume 4, July 2008, p. 152. https://pdfs.semanticscholar.org/c952/cb2af81932570fe28fcd-be0a6895694d17bc.pdf
24 Hutchins, Francis G., op. cit., p. 66.
25 Fischer, Louis, op. cit., pp. 328–329.
26 Buber, Martin, "Open Letter to Gandhi", https://www.jewishvirtuallibrary.org/letter-from-martin-buber-to-gandhi, accessed June 6, 2020.
27 Ibid.
28 Panter-Brick, Simone, op. cit., p. 122.
29 Arendt, Hannah, *On Violence*, New York, Harcourt & Brace, 1969, p. 53.

CONCLUSION
Gandhi and the future of peace

For Gandhi, violence was the sign of the failure of legitimate political power. This was the core of Gandhi's political theory – a view of politics as shaped by an internal moral power, rather than from the standpoint of a rational instrumentalism. Unlike Max Weber, who considered the modern state as "a human community which (successfully) lays claim to the claim of legitimate physical violence within a certain territory,"[1] Gandhi's search for excellence in politics was a powerful manner to make possible the fullest development of human personality. Consequently, for Gandhi, the modern state contained forces that threatened rather than enhance liberty. Therefore, Gandhi did not consider democracy but as a value, which needed to be created and cherished. Therefore, his defence of the institutions of the liberal constitutional state did not mean that he justified them in terms of his political philosophy. Quite the contrary, politics for Gandhi was an act of consciousness, not a mode of living taken for granted. Gandhi did not glorify political action as the immediate capture of political office. According to Gandhi, the basic condition of political action was the elimination of violence. Gandhi's principal aim was to civilize modern politics from within, by shorting the circuit of resentment, hatred and coercion. Actually, one can describe his efforts in politics of nonviolence as a method to mobilize collective power in a manner that attends to its own moral education in an exemplary and innovative way. If Gandhi's political philosophy has any lesson to teach us, it is the following: excellence is the end that we have to set before ourselves as political beings. Gandhi's argument was to show that a life in excellence is an agency and a transformative force, a lived experience underpinning the work of peacemaking and cross-fertilization of cultures.

For the Greeks, human excellence in general characterized the *kalos kagathos*, the noble and good man. But this nobility of spirit was considered possible only in the context of the polis, the city-state, because it is an ethos that excels towards public virtue. That is why *paideia* was the education through which excellence was fostered. To the Greeks the supreme task of man, therefore, was to discover what human "excellence" is and to achieve it; and *paideia* traced the steps of the discovery and the growing process and enrichment of the human ideal. The Greeks believed that excellence breeds excellence. So striving for excellence for its own sake, for truth, beauty and goodness in the whole educational process, was considered as the only way to produce it. In the same manner, for Gandhi, attaining moral and political excellence represented the social spirit that came from a maturation of man's innate sense of fellowship and gentleness and that extended beyond civility and good manners to a broader sense of empathy that made possible a peaceful and nonviolent way of life in an orderly and harmonious society. Gandhi knew well that to attain peace, individuals and societies needed to attain excellence by achieving a balance of moral virtue and righteousness. Hegel would call this a "learning process" (*Bildung*). From Gandhi's point of view, this learning process was at the same time a dynamic to create strong sense of empathy for other human beings as citizens of human history.

Gandhi was well aware of the fact that world peace is a difficult and daunting task. But he also knew that it is a never-ending quest for excellence and exemplarity. It is the thin distance that humankind has placed between itself and barbarism. Gandhi knew well that if human beings wanted to attain world peace, they had to believe in political life as excellence. Moreover, his point was that peace is its own excellence. As a matter of fact, Gandhi saw peace and nonviolence primarily as choices concerning individual's own conscience. Gandhi actually provided an argument in favour of nonviolent peace as "ethic of responsibility," in the Weberian sense of the term, as a framework for monitoring socio-political action. It goes without saying that for Gandhi violence is the worst sin of the politician. By extension, we can say that for him, violence is also the greatest sin of action. As such, Gandhi argued for a dedicated and committed political ethos, which did not accept the necessity of "dirty hands" in politics. As he affirmed on July 3, 1940,

> I have always derived my politics from ethics or religion and my strength is also derived by my deriving my politics from ethics. It is also because I swear by ethics and religion that I find myself in politics. A person who is a lover of his country is bound to take lively interest in politics, otherwise he will not be able to carry on his avocation with peace.[2]

Gandhi was thinking in terms of long-term social stability among nations, so he wanted to put his hands on the wheel of history through nonviolent peace. But for Gandhi, the ethic of responsibility present in the process of peacemaking included the recognition of the Otherness of the Other. Ultimately, what was important for Gandhi was to move from violence to politics. This transition could not take place without the intervention of the ethical into the political. In a speech at All-India National Education Conference on January 13, 1930, Gandhi observed:

> There are some who think that morality has nothing to do with politics. We do not concern ourselves with the character of our leaders...If swaraj was not meant to civilize us, and to purify and stabilize our civilization, it would be nothing worth. The very essence of our civilization is that we give a paramount place to morality in all our affairs, public or private.[3]

The Gandhian appeal to the ethical on the path of peace was not only a way to seek for Truth but also that of coming to know oneself in ever greater depth. In one word, the Gandhian effort for peacemaking was an inwardly cultivation of one's capacity to be compassionate. In other words, as it has been underlined previously, Gandhi considered peace as also a work of the heart and not only that of reason. This is a reminder of the famous quote by the French philosopher Pascal, who said: "The heart has its reasons which reason itself does not know."[4] In the same manner, Gandhi believed that the heart, and not reason, is the seat of morality. As he writes in *Harijan* on June 8, 1940, "Morality which depends upon the helplessness of a man or woman has not much to recommend it. Morality is rooted in the purity of our hearts."[5] In other words, Gandhi believed that next to constructive work, a society needs also to be inwardly empowered, since human beings are not only practitioners of wars and conflicts but they are also capable of love, friendship, solidarity and empathy. Gandhi was thinking of a humanity which could transcend the rule of violence and confront it with the only thing at its disposal: its moral nature. Gandhi was aware of this truth few years before he started his non-cooperation campaign in Indian. On January 5, 1907, he wrote the following in the columns of the *Indian Opinion*:

> It is the moral nature of man by which he rises to good and noble thoughts. The different sciences show us the world as it is. Ethics tells us what it ought to be. It enables man to know how he should act. Man has two windows to his mind: through one he can see his own self as it is; through the other, he can see what it ought to be. It is our task to analyse and explore the body, the brain and the mind of man separately; but if we stop here, we derive no benefit despite our scientific knowledge. It is necessary to know about the evil effects of injustice, wickedness, vanity and the like, and the disaster they spell where the three are found together. And mere knowledge is not enough, it should be followed by appropriate action. An ethical idea is like an architect's plan. The plan shows how the building should be constructed; but it becomes useless if the building is not raised accordingly. Similarly, an ethical idea is useless so long as it is not followed by suitable action.... In the path

of morality there is no such thing as reward for moral behaviour. If a man does some good deed, he does not do it to win applause, he does it because he must. For him doing good is but a higher kind of food, if one may compare food and goodness.[6]

It is crucial for our understanding of Gandhi's vision of world peace to realize the significance of a moral act as a basic principle in striving to fashion and promote peace. Moreover, Gandhi, unlike many modern theorists, insisted on the autonomous nature of the moral act. Hence he was most categorical by saying that:

A moral act must be our own act; it must spring from our own will. If we act mechanically, there is no moral content in our act. Such action would be moral, if we think it proper to act like a machine and do so. For in doing so, we use our discrimination. We should bear in mind the distinction between acting mechanically and acting intentionally. It may be a moral of a king to pardon a culprit. But the messenger bearing the order of pardon plays only a mechanical part in the king's moral act…. Just as a moral action should be free from fear or compulsion so should there be no self-interest behind it. This is not to say that actions prompted by self-interest are all worthless, but only that to call them moral would detract from the [dignity of the] moral idea.[7]

Seeking to provide an alternative vision to the utilitarian and materialistic modernity, Gandhi upheld the idea that an immoral modernity has a tendency to produce wars and conflicts. He stroke an emotional chord with his readers and followers when he called war "a disciplined destruction" and a "demoniac non-cooperation."[8] However, Gandhi was thoroughly convinced that his own strategy of non-cooperation was moral and "divine." He wrote:

I do not think that I am being guilty of presumption in claiming that the non-cooperation I am placing before

CONCLUSION

the country is of a divine type...In non-cooperation of the divine type, effort is never fruitless, nor is there any question of moral taint.[9]

Now we have some understanding of why Gandhi developed insights into the interrelatedness of morality and politics. In this sense, Gandhi's view of morality was not a denial of politics; quite the contrary, Gandhi's experiments with morality were taking place in the public realm. His moral idealism was completed by a political realism, which hoped for the construction of world peace. Gandhi wrote, "I feel that political work must be looked upon in terms of social and moral progress."[10] Gandhi's vision of peace was a powerful reminder of the tragic disjunction of politics and ethics. For Gandhi, the horrors of World War II and the danger of a nuclear war further strengthened his conviction that peace is reached only by the power of love and soul force. Less than two years before his assassination, he advised his readers of the dangers of the advent of a new war. "If the third war comes," he wrote in *Harijan* on December 6, 1946, "it will be the end of the world. The world cannot stand a third war, For me the second war has not stopped, it still goes on."[11]

Gandhi struggled all his life to transform the ideas of hatred and war into a belief in nonviolence and peace. More than seventy years after, he still stands high as an iconic figure for peace. Peacemakers throughout the world have found in him an inspiration and a milestone in their battles for peacemaking. In this worldwide battle for peace, three names stand out: Martin Luther King, Jr., Nelson Mandela and His Holiness the Dalai Lama. King's appreciation of interconnectedness of human beings was directly linked to the challenge of peace in the world. The manner King criticized the war in Vietnam was closely related to his approach concerning the transformation of the social, political and economic structures of injustice around the globe. Inspired by Mahatma Gandhi's philosophy of nonviolence and peace, he wrote:

> What must they think of the United States of America when they realize that we permitted the repression and

> cruelty of Diem, which helped to bring them into being as a resistance group in the South? What do they think of our condoning the violence which led to their own taking up of arms? How can they believe in our integrity when now we speak of "aggression from the North" as if there was nothing more essential to the war? How can they trust us when now we charge them with violence after the murderous reign of Diem and charge them with violence while we pour every new weapon of death into their land?[12]

As such, King established philosophical grounds for an ethos of peace by meeting the Gandhian imperatives. In the face of a harsh conflict in Vietnam, he appealed to the Gandhian and Christian doctrines of peacemaking and reconciliation in order to conquer the evil of war. Ultimately, for King, the process of peacemaking had to be just and compassionate. In other words, peace had to reflect the moral law of the universe. Also, against the arrogance of war, King suggested the two imperatives of justice and morality. Therefore, from King's point of view, peace, as a moral institution, was on the side of conviviality and fellowship. But, King knew well that in order for peace to be convivial and compassionate, it needed to be empathetic towards the others, starting with all those who were suffering from the Great Power diplomacy.

> King interpreted the interrelatedness of human existence to mean that "injustice anywhere is a threat to justice everywhere" because injustice has a corporate effect. He believed that the denial of constitutional rights to anyone potentially violated the rights of all citizens...As a result of his solidaristic approach to human existence King believed that the civil rights movement was contributing more to the national life than simply the elimination of racial injustice.[13]

As such, King envisioned peacemaking both as struggle and as solidarity. He wanted people to feel solidarity for their adversaries

CONCLUSION

in the same way as they felt for their families and friends. If the universe was just and righteous, then behind the struggle for righteousness resided what King called a "cosmic companionship."[14] King had an immense faith in human interconnectedness as the cure for war and violence. In his views, it was disunity and indifference which represented the causes of hatred, vengeance and conflict. In a Gandhian manner, all of King's ethical and political concerns for peace were directed to the priority he assigned to the idea of recognition of one's indebtedness to others. As King later wrote:

> We are everlasting debtors to known and unknown men and women. We do not finish breakfast without being dependent on more than half of the world. When we arise in the morning, we go into the bathroom where we reach for a sponge which is provided for us by a Pacific Islander. We reach for soap that is created for us by a Frenchman. The towel is provided by a Turk. Then at the table we drink coffee which is provided for us by a South American, or tea by a Chinese, or cocoa by a West African. Before we leave for our jobs we are beholden to more than half the world. In a real sense, all life is interrelated. All men are caught in an inescapable network of mutuality, tied in a single garment of destiny. Whatever affects one directly affects all indirectly.[15]

Nelson Mandela could also be considered as a Gandhian leader who cherished the ideal of a world peace all his life. Consequently, Mandela accumulated his moral capital as a leader through his empathetic ethics and with a self-conscious respect for peace. That is why, there were certainly moments in Mandela's life when his character as a moral leader and as a global peacemaker came closer to the Gandhian ideal of peace. It is with this Gandhian spirit in mind that Mandela accepted to join hands with his enemies in order to drag South Africa out of hatred and bloodshed, but also to be the African ambassador of peace. Mandela was brought up with the African philosophy of *ubuntu*, which described a quality of empathy and compassion.

CONCLUSION

It was therefore not surprising that when Mandela assumed the presidency in 1994, South Africa's foreign policy continued the legacy formulated by the older generation and was defined by the notion of "a better Africa and a better world." Mandela prioritized these fundamental, *ubuntu*-inspired values as essential to cultivating a humane foreign policy.[16]

Despite all his critics on the Right and on the Left, Mandela never abandoned his Gandhian view of peace. If Mandela is celebrated today as a political leader with a moral legacy, it is mainly because his politics of national and international reconciliation is more relevant than ever for all those who continue to believe in a world without wars and conflicts. In his Nobel Peace Prize Acceptance Lecture on December 10, 1993, Mandela developed his Gandhian approach to peace. He affirmed:

> We stand here today as nothing more than a representative of the millions of our people who dared to rise up against a social system whose very essence is war, violence, racism, oppression, repression and the impoverishment of an entire people. I am also here today as a representative of the millions of people across the globe, the anti-apartheid movement, the governments and organisations that joined with us, not to fight against South Africa as a country or any of its peoples, but to oppose an inhuman system and sue for a speedy end to the apartheid crime against humanity. These countless human beings, both inside and outside our country, had the nobility of spirit to stand in the path of tyranny and injustice, without seeking selfish gain. They recognised that an injury to one is an injury to all and therefore acted together in defense of justice and a common human decency. Because of their courage and persistence for many years, we can, today, even set the dates when all humanity will join together to celebrate one of the outstanding human victories of our century. Let it never be said by future generations that indifference, cynicism

CONCLUSION

or selfishness made us fail to live up to the ideals of humanism which the Nobel Peace Prize encapsulates. Let the strivings of us all, prove Martin Luther King Jr. to have been correct, when he said that humanity can no longer be tragically bound to the starless midnight of racism and war. Let the efforts of us all, prove that he was not a mere dreamer when he spoke of the beauty of genuine brotherhood and peace being more precious than diamonds or silver or gold.[17]

Tenzin Gyatso, His Holiness the Dalai Lama, the fourteenth in title, is the last prophet of peace alive. Since Mahatma Gandhi's death in January 1948, no one has exerted a greater influence than His Holiness the Dalai Lama on the philosophy of peace around the world, in ways different from those of a Martin Luther King, Jr., or Nelson Mandela. The Dalai Lama's message is, therefore, very clear: men are all naturally good, but they ignore their true nature, because they hide it behind the mask of violence and hatred. So His Holiness is inviting us to trust our nature, because it teaches us that there is

> a goodness engraved deep within us, a fundamental and all-powerful gentleness .... Goodness that extends to the whole universe and that will one day lead us to nirvana, but a fragile goodness, since the murder of a dog can disturb the order of the world. Secret goodness too, is easily concealed under the arrogance, brutality and greed that are the masks we most often wear.[18]

Peace is, therefore, for the Dalai Lama a *de facto* recognition of the Other. By "the Other," His Holiness the Dalai Lama means every living element which is part of this universal harmony. This is why he declares that "the killing of an animal is an attack on universal harmony."[19] This universal harmony can be summed up by the notion of "interdependence" as taught by the Buddha. For the Dalai Lama, as in the case of Gandhi and King, peace is the manifestation of a common humanity. His Holiness explains this in the following:

CONCLUSION

We have a further quality which is central to our identity as human beings; our instinctive capacity for empathy. Of course we are not alone in this. Some other animals exhibit behavior that seems to indicate empathy. Nonetheless, it is an essential human trait...We naturally enjoy empathetic experience and often seek it in our lives.[20]

For his Holiness the Dalai Lama, peace is part of the empathetic nature of human beings, because there is no such thing as an isolated self. Humankind is part of the universe just like any other species and must maintain its harmony through peace and compassion. Peace and compassion, therefore, are indispensable qualities for the fellowship of humankind with the universe. The solution that His Holiness suggests for the world peace is not very different from the "integral humanism" of Mahatma Gandhi. From the Dalai Lama's point of view, the two concepts of compassion and responsibility are key ideas in bringing humanity to a stage of consciousness on peace. According to His Holiness,

> One nation's problems can no longer be satisfactorily solved by itself alone; too much depends on the interest, attitude, and cooperation of other nations. A universal humanitarian approach to world problems seems the only sound basis for world peace... Although the increasing interdependence among nations might be expected to generate more sympathetic cooperation, it is difficult to achieve a spirit of genuine cooperation as long as people remain indifferent to the feelings and happiness of others. When people are motivated mostly by greed and jealousy, it is not possible for them to live in harmony... Living in society, we should share the sufferings of our fellow citizens and practise compassion and tolerance not only towards our loved ones but also towards our enemies. This is the test of our moral strength. We must set an example by our own practice, for we cannot hope to convince others of the value of religion by mere words. We must live up to the same high standards of integrity and sacrifice that we ask of others. The ultimate purpose

> of all religions is to serve and benefit humanity. This is why it is so important that religion always be used to effect the happiness and peace of all beings and not merely to convert others.[21]

For His Holiness the Dalai Lama, compassion and the practice of peace are not elitist choices, but the only choices possible in our everyday actions, because of the equivalence they establish between the ends and the means. As such, he believes that if peace and nonviolence are expressed in our everyday actions, then the challenge before us is to be able to reflect on the means. As such, Dalai Lama's application of the Gandhian moment of nonviolence is also the acceptance of the fact that peace is not always immediately around the corner. According to the Dalai Lama, we need to combine and harmonize peacemaking with spiritual growth.

As it has been pointed out in the previous chapter, Mahatma Gandhi was very attentive of the fact that world peace is not possible without spiritual growth of humanity. So far, of the 21st century, just two decades have gone, and they have not been peaceful. As a result, many among the human population around the world believe that humanity will never attain peace. But we all know that peace is the result of a long process of compassionate dialogue and tireless caring. Peace cannot emerge without believing in peace. If we don't get tired and don't give up our pursuit of peace, it will be well with us at the end. But who says "peace" says "peaceful coexistence," which takes us to the idea of one humanity and one world. We frustrate our destiny if we continue to base our hopes on a world of divisions, hatreds and sectarian quarrels, each of us arrogating to ourselves the larger share, if not the monopoly, of national, civilizational and moral superiority. The path to peace is, therefore, that of cosmopolitan conversations across cultural, religious and political boundaries. It is generally recognized that Gandhi's conception of nonviolence as a moral and political ideal places him in the cosmopolitan tradition. From Gandhi's perspective, nonviolence is an ontological truth that follows from the unity and interdependence of humanity and life. While violence damages and undermines all forms of life, nonviolence uplifts all. Gandhi, therefore, advocated an awareness of the essential unity of humanity, and that awareness required a critical self-examination and a move from egocentricity towards a "shared humanity." This "shared humanity" cannot exist today if it is not aware of its own shortcomings. It needs to strive to remove its own imperfections in order to be able to foster a pluralistic peace. Needless to say that in an age of increasing "globalization of selfishness," there is an urgent need to read and practise the Gandhian social and political philosophy in order re-evaluate the concept of peace. More clearly, Gandhi's nonviolent perspective of peace presents itself as a dynamic balance between the ethical imperative of respecting the Otherness of the Other and the principle of the recognition of a common humanity. It is a farsighted process of peacemaking which seriously advocates a dialogical world citizenship beyond national selfishness and global exclusion. Gandhi had great faith in the power of peace. And he had faith in the exemplary life of peacemakers. With an awareness of the significance of his philosophy for our world comes, gradually but surely, an appreciation of his devotion to world peace.

Notes

1 Weber, Max, "The Profession and Vocation of Politics," in *Political Writings*, Cambridge University Press, Cambridge, 1994, pp. 310–311.
2 Gandhi, Mahatma, *The Collected Works of Mahatma Gandhi*, op. cit., vol. 72, 1978, p. 243.
3 Gandhi, Mahatma, *The Collected Works of Mahatma Gandhi*, op. cit., vol. 42, 1970, p. 395.
4 Pascal, Blaise, *Pensées and Other Writings*, Oxford University Press, Oxford, 2008, p. 158.
5 Gandhi, Mahatma, *The Collected Works of Mahatma Gandhi*, op. cit., vol. 72, 1978, p. 137.
6 Gandhi, Mahatma, *The Collected Works of Mahatma Gandhi*, op. cit., vol. 6, 1961, p. 275.
7 Ibid., vol. 6, pp. 284–285.
8 Gandhi, Mahatma, *The Collected Works of Mahatma Gandhi*, op. cit., vol. 18, 1965, pp. 240, 126.
9 Ibid., p. 126.
10 Gandhi, Mahatma, *The Collected Works of Mahatma Gandhi*, op. cit., vol. 85, 1982, p. 368.

CONCLUSION

11 Ibid., p. 370.
12 King, Martin Luther, Jr., *A Testament of Hope: The Essential Writings of Martin Luther King, Jr.*, edited by James Melvin Washington, Harper & Row, New York, 1986, pp. 236–237.
13 Smith, Kenneth L. & Zepp, Ira G., *Search for the Beloved Community: The Thinking of Martin Luther King, Jr.*, Judson Press, Valley Forge, 1974, p. 122.
14 King, Martin Luther, Jr., *A Testament of Hope*, op. cit., p. 40.
15 King, Martin Luther, Jr., *Where Do We Go From Here: Chaos or Community?* Harper & Row, New York, 1967, p. 181.
16 Ndlovu, Sifiso M. "Mandela's Presidential Years: An Africanist View", in Barnard, Rita (ed.) *Cambridge Companion to Nelson Mandela*, Cambridge University Press, New York, 2014, p. 193.
17 Mandela, Nelson, Nobel Acceptance Lecture, in https://www.nobelprize.org/prizes/peace/1993/mandela/26130-nelson-mandela-nobel-lecture-1993/, accessed June 6, 2020.
18 Le Dalaï-Lama, Carrière, Jean-Claude, Robert *Laffont, La force du bouddhisme*, Paris, 1994, p. 182 (translated by the author).
19 Ibid., p. 181.
20 His Holiness the Dalai Lama, *Beyond Religion: Ethics for a Whole World*, Harper Element, New Delhi, 2015, p. 26.
21 His Holiness the Dalai Lama, *A Human Approach to World Peace*, https://www.dalailama.com/messages/world-peace/a-human-approach-to-world-peace, accessed June 6, 2020.

BIBLIOGRAPHY

Allen, Douglas, *The Philosophy of Mahatma Gandhi for the Twenty-First Century*, Oxford University Press, New Delhi, 2009.
Arendt, Hannah, *On Violence*, Harcourt & Brace, New York, 1969.
Ashu Pasricha, Ashu & Misra, R.P., *Rediscovering Gandhi*, Volume 4, Concensual Democracy: Gandhi on State Power and Politics Concept Publishing Company, New Delhi, 2010.
Barnard, Rita, *Cambridge Companion to Nelson Mandela*, Cambridge University Press, New York, 2014.
Bondurant, J. (ed), *Harijan: Collected Issues of Gandhi's Journals, 1933-1955*, 19 Volumes, Garland Publishing, New York, 1973.
Bose, Nirmal Kumar (ed), *Selections from Gandhi*, Navajivan Publishing, Ahmedabad, 1968.
Brown, Judith M., *Gandhi: Prisoner of Hope*, Yale University Press, New Haven, CT, 1989.
Chadha, Yogesh, *Rediscovering Gandhi*, Century Books, London, 1997.
Chakrabarty, Bidyut, *Social and Political Thought of Mahatma Gandhi*, Routledge, Oxon, 2006.
Dhawan, Gopinath, *The Philosophy of Mahatma Gandhi*, Navajivan Publishing, Ahmedabad, 1957.
Fischer, Louis, *The Essential Gandhi: His Life, Work and Ideas*, Vintage Books, New York, 1963.
Gandhi, Mahatma, *All Men are Brothers: Life and Thoughts of Mahatma Gandhi as Told in His Own Words*, edited by Kripalani, Krishna, Navajivan Publishing House, Ahmedabad, 1971.
Gandhi, Mahatma, *An Autobiography or The Story of My Experiments with Truth*, translated from the Gujarati by Mashadev Desai, Navajivan Publishing House, Ahmedabad, 1927.

BIBLIOGRAPHY

Gandhi, Mahatma, *Collected Works of Mahatma Gandhi*, Volume 72, Publications Division Government of India, New Delhi, 1999.

Gandhi, Mahatma, *The Essential Writings*, Oxford University Press, Oxford, 2008.

Gandhi, Mahatma, *From Yeravda Mandir*, Navajivan Publishing, Ahmedabad, 1937.

Gandhi, Mahatma, *Gandhi: An Autobiography*, Beacon Press, Boston, 1957.

Gandhi, Mahatma, *Nonviolent Resistance*, Schocken, New York, 1961.

Gandhi, Mahatma, *Selected Political Writings*, edited by Dennis Dalton, Hackett Publishing, Indianapolis, IN, 1996.

Gandhi, Rajmohan, *Mohandas: A True Story of a Man, His People and an Empire*, Penguin –Viking, New Delhi, 2006.

Gangal, Suresh Chandra, *The Gandhian Way to World Peace*, Vora & Co. Publishers, Bombay, 1960.

Gonsalves, Peter, *Clothing for Liberation: A Communication Analysis of Gandhi's Swadeshi Revolution*, Sage Publications, New Delhi, 2010.

His Holiness the Dalai Lama, *Beyond Religion: Ethics for a Whole World*, Harper Element, New Delhi, 2015.

Hutchins, Francis G., *Gandhi's Battlefield Choice: The Mahatma, The Bhagavad Gita and World War II*, Manohar, New Delhi, 2017.

Kant, Immanuel, *An Answer to the Question: What Is Enlightenment?* Great Ideas, Penguin Books, London, 2009.

King, Martin Luther, Jr., *A Testament of Hope*, Harper & Row Publishers, San Francisco, CA, 1986.

King, Martin Luther, Jr., "I Have a Dream" in *Writings and Speeches that Changed the World*, Baker & Taylor, CATS, Charlotte, NC, 2009.

King, Martin Luther, Jr., *Where Do We Go from Here: Chaos or Community?* Harper & Row, New York, 1967.

Le Dalaï-Lama, Carrière, Jean-Claude & Robert Laffont, *La force du bouddhisme*, Robert Laffont, Paris, 1994.

Mazmudar, B., *Gandhiji's Non-violence in Theory and Practice*, Mani Bhavan Gandhi Sangrahalaya, Mumbai, 2003.

Merton, Thomas, *Gandhi on Nonviolence*, Speaking Tiger, New Delhi, 2016.

Parekh, Bhikhu, *Colonialism, Tradition and Reform: An Analysis of Gandhi's Political Discourse*, Sage Publications, New Delhi, 1989.

Parel, Anthony & Brown, Judith M., *The Cambridge Companion to Gandhi*, Cambridge University Press, New Delhi, 2011.

BIBLIOGRAPHY

Pascal, Blaise, *Pensées and Other Writings*, Oxford University Press, Oxford, 2008.

Pfostel, Eva, *Between Ethics and Politics: Gandhi Today*, Routledge, New Delhi, 2014.

Radakrishnan, S., *Mahatma Gandhi 100 Years*, Gandhi Peace Foundation, New Delhi, 1968.

Richards, Glyn, *The Philosophy of Gandhi: A Study of His Basic Ideas*, Curzon Press, Totowa, 1982.

Smith, Kenneth L. & Zepp, Ira G., *Search for the Beloved Community: The Thinking of Martin Luther King, Jr.*, Judson Press, Valley Forge, 1974.

Tendulkar, Dinanath Gopal, *Mahatma; Life of Mohandas Karamchand Gandhi*, Ministry of Information and Braodcasting Government of India, New Delhi, 1961 (1951).

Weber, Max, *Political Writings*, Cambridge University Press, Cambridge, 1994.

For Product Safety Concerns and Information please contact our EU representative GPSR@taylorandfrancis.com
Taylor & Francis Verlag GmbH, Kaufingerstraße 24, 80331 München, Germany

www.ingramcontent.com/pod-product-compliance
Lightning Source LLC
Chambersburg PA
CBHW061720300426
44115CB00014B/2767